A Time for Prayer

Publications International, Ltd.

Let's get social!

 @Publications_International

 @PublicationsInternational

www.pilbooks.com

Table of Contents

A Time for Prayer

Hear my prayer, O Lord,
give ear to my supplications:
in thy faithfulness answer me,
and in thy righteousness.

—Psalm 143:1

A Time for Prayer is a collection of reflections, prayers, Bible verses, and devotionals for every day of the year. We hope they will inspire you and enrich your days and nights.

Holy, Holy, Holy! Lord God Almighty!

Holy, holy, holy! Lord God almighty!
Early in the morning our song shall rise to thee;
Holy, holy, holy! merciful and mighty!
God in three persons, blessed Trinity!

Holy, holy, holy! All the saints adore thee,
Casting down their golden crowns around the glassy sea;
Cherubim and seraphim falling down before thee,
Which wert, and art, and evermore shalt be.

Holy, holy, holy! Though the darkness hide thee,
Though the eye of sinful man, thy glory may not see:
Only thou art holy, there is none beside thee,
Perfect in power, in love, and purity.

Holy, holy, holy! Lord God almighty!
All thy works shall praise thy name in earth, and sky, and sea;
Holy, holy, holy! Merciful and mighty,
God in three persons, blessed Trinity!

—Reginald Heber

January

January 1

Lord, speak to me through these pages.
Let me hear your gentle words
Come whispering through the ages
And thundering through the world.

Challenge me and change me,
comfort me and calm me.
Completely rearrange me,
Soothe me with a psalm.

Teach me how to please you,
Show me how to live.
Inspire me to praise you
For all the love you give.

January 2

Lord, it is tempting and easy to cast a scornful eye on those around us and note every fault. When my pride tempts me to do so, prompt me to turn the magnifying glass on myself instead. If I keep in mind how much I need your forgiveness every day, my love for you will never grow cold. I know you are willing to forgive each and every fault if I only ask.

January 3

God, make me an open vessel through which the waters of your Spirit flow freely. Let your love move through me and out into my world, touching everyone I come in contact with. Express your joy through the special talents you have given me, that others may come to know your presence in their own lives by witnessing your presence in mine. Amen.

January 4

The past does not have to be an enemy. Rather, let it be a friend and an ally that reminds you of where you've been, how far you've come, and what you've learned along the way. Then let it go as you would a favorite but little-used old garment, with love and gratitude, knowing that God will always provide you with something wonderful and new to wear along the way.

January 5

> *For he shall give his angels charge over thee,*
> *to keep thee in all thy ways.*
>
> *–Psalm 91:11*

Angels are yet one more sign of God's goodness, a sign that God cares for us and uses many ways to express that love. Many people find peace in knowing that angels are watching.

January 6

Lord, why is it that we see the faults of others so clearly but ignore our own until the pile gets so big, we finally trip over it? We desire to be more gracious than we are, Lord. Just as you have showered us with kindness and forgiveness, help us to do the same for those around us. Speak to our hearts, Lord. Open them and fill them with compassion.

January 7

The fearful mind sees limitations and accepts them as obstacles that cannot be overcome. The inspired mind sees those same limitations and accepts them as challenges— challenges that can become opportunities to move out beyond the comfort zone and into a realm of pure potential and limitless possibility.

January 8

Father, we try to live modestly and not flaunt our belongings before those who have less. But our children are surrounded by playmates who pile up possessions only to tire of them and quickly discard them. Our children are envious and think they, too, need the latest toys and the trendiest clothes.

How can we convince them that things can't make them happy? How do we instill in them the values that will make their lives fulfilling? Help us, O Lord, to plant in their hearts yearnings for the important things in life, such as friendships, love for God, healthy bodies, creative minds, and helping hearts.

Our children are our most valued treasures. Humbly we commend them to your care.

January 9

When we think of joy, we often think of things that are new—a new day, a new baby, a new love, a new beginning, the promise of a new home with God in heaven. Rejoicing in these things originates with having joy in the God who makes all things new. Rather than relying on earthly pleasures to provide happiness, the Scriptures command that we rejoice in God and in each new day he brings. Joy is a celebration of the heart that goes beyond circumstances to the very foundation of joy—the knowledge that we are loved by God.

January 10

Father in heaven, sometimes I feel anger welling up inside me, and I need to turn to you for counsel. Please stay near to me and help me to find ways to express my emotions without harming another's feelings or getting myself so upset I cannot see past my own feelings. I need to understand myself, express myself, and accept myself—all within the bounds of your teachings. Amen.

January 11

Just when all seems hopeless, prayer lifts us like a wave on the ocean. A sturdy craft, prayer doesn't hide from pain, but uses it like the force of the sea to move us to a new place of insight, patience, courage, and sympathy. Always, it is God's hand beneath the surface holding us up.

January 12

To have talent and not use it is to ignore the calling of a higher voice. To be given gifts and not share them is to nullify the moving of spirit through the soul as it seeks to be made manifest in the outer world. We are given our light to let it shine, not to hide it from others for fear of drawing attention. For when we shine, we allow others to do so as well. God did not make stars in order to keep them from glowing in the night sky, nor did he make birds in order to keep them grounded. When we open our storehouse of talents and treasures, the whole world benefits and is made brighter.

January 13

From the dark night of the soul
Comes the blessing of the dawn.
From the deep wounds of the heart
Comes the gift of love reborn.
From the chaos of confusion
Comes the calm of clarity.
From the anguish of discord
Comes the peace of harmony.
From the grieving of great loss
Comes the happiness of new life.
From the coldness of despair
Comes the warmth of our Father's light.

January 14

Everything looks much brighter than it did before. My prayer for strength has been answered. My cries for help have been heard. My pleas for mercy flew directly to your throne. Now I'm ready to help my neighbor, Lord. Let me not delay.

January 15

Today I want to spend time with you, renewing Spirit.
In fact, I'd like to spend the whole day just being in your presence.
For this one day I will not worry about the work I
have to do or the goals I want to accomplish.
I will pull back and simply listen for your guidance.
I'm willing to change my life in order to fit your perfect will,
and I ask that you begin that work in my heart, even now.
I'll let go of personal ambition, for now.
I'll loosen my grip on the things I've wanted to
accomplish and the recognition I've craved for so long.
All of this I give over to you.
I'm content to be a servant for now, quiet and
unnoticed, if that is what you desire.
I'm even willing to be misunderstood, if you will only
respond to my sincere prayer for a renewed heart.
Thank you. I need you so much.

January 16

And out of the ground the Lord God formed every beast of the field, and every fowl of the air; and brought them unto Adam to see what he would call them: and whatsoever Adam called every living creature, that was the name thereof.

—Genesis 2:19

Thank you, God, for all the animals who have helped us to feel closer to you and your creation. Keep them safe, these trusted innocents who calm our lives and show us love. Help them find their way home if they are lost. Help them hear the voices of those who will care for them. Save them from every unsafe place.

January 17

Every moment we are alive is full of reasons to sing out in joyful gratitude. Every breath we are given is a reminder that the glory of life is at hand. In the people we love, in the beauty of nature, in the golden sun that rises each morning—miracles are every-where.

January 18

Lord, look down upon my family with merciful eyes, and help us to heal the divides that threaten to grow between us. Guide us toward the solutions that will empower everyone involved, and remind us that we work better when we work together. Help us to speak honestly with each other. Amen.

January 19

There is plenty of evidence for the existence of God, but if we could absolutely prove it, faith wouldn't be necessary. Even with all the evidence of creation and the soul, God left room for us to be free beings. Freedom is what brings such creativity, invention, and interest to the world.

January 20

> *For if ye forgive men their*
> *trespasses, your heavenly Father*
> *will also forgive you.*
>
> —*Matthew 6:14*

Mercy is a beautiful word, Father. I breathe a sigh of relief just thinking about your mercy toward me. Help me to remember that—as the recipient of such generous forgiveness—I should be quick to forgive others, whether I am the victim of a minor thoughtless slight or some bigger affront.

Let us search and try our ways,
and turn again to the Lord.

—*Lamentations 3:40*

I am like two halves of a walnut, God. I
am of two minds: despairing and hopeful.
Help me to feel your hand holding me
together as I rebuild my life when at first
it seemed too hard to even try. In order to
get to the meat of a walnut, it must be split
into halves. May the brokenness I feel get
me to the nourishment—the meat—I need
in order to move on. Amen.

January 22

Lord, you are here,
Lord, you are there.
You are wherever we go.

Lord, you guide us,
Lord, you protect us.
You are wherever we go.

Lord, we need you,
Lord, we trust you,
You are wherever we go.

Lord, we love you,
Lord, we praise you,
You are wherever we go.

January 23

> *Beareth all things, believeth all things, hopeth all things, endureth all things.*
>
> *—1 Corinthians 13:7*

There are many events in our lives over which we have no control. However, we do have a choice either to endure trying times and press on or to give up. The secret of survival, whether or not we question God's presence or his ability to help us, is remembering that our hope is in the fairness, goodness, and justice of God. When we put our trust in the character of a God who cannot fail us, we will remain faithful. Our trust and faithfulness produce the endurance that sees us through the "tough stuff" we all face in this life.

January 24

> *As every man hath received the gift,*
> *even so minister the same one to another,*
> *as good stewards of the manifold*
> *grace of God.*
>
> *–1 Peter 4:10*

One of my friends is going through a difficult time, and I don't know what to do. I feel so helpless. You know his needs, Lord, better than I do. I hold him up to you in prayer. If there is some way you can use me to help him, I ask that you plant the idea in my head. I ask that any words I say to him be inspired by you.

January 25

Loving God, I have dedicated my children to you and have promised to teach them your laws. Sometimes I feel ineloquent, inadequate, unfit for the task. But you are with me, Lord; you can supply what I lack.

I long to show my loved ones how to walk daily in your light, to bask in your warmth, and to love you with all of their hearts.

Please grant me the understanding I need to show each child how to worship and obey you, so they may experience the joy of your presence in their lives.

Your love fills me with song, O Lord. Help me teach the words to my children.

January 26

I always want to be a dreamer, O God, to feel the stir and the yearning to see my vision become reality. There are those who would say dreamers are free-floaters. When I dream I feel connected to you and to your creation, bound by purpose and a sense of call. Nourish my dreams and my striving to make them real.

January 27

How good to get this promotion! And how I've waited for this day! Now that it is here, I thank you for the chance to savor it. A job well done is a good thing, I know. I will celebrate before your smiling eyes and give you credit, too. Because, after all, everything I am and have comes from your gracious hand.

January 28

> *And thou shalt put some of thine honor upon him, that all the congregation of the children of Israel may be obedient.*
>
> *–Numbers 27:20*

Dear heavenly Father, today, if I see or hear of someone who is struggling in some way, please help me take a moment to remember what it was like when I was struggling and you helped me through the aid of a friend or stranger. Let that memory mobilize me to offer help and be your true servant. This I pray. Amen.

January 29

Some prayers are best left unfinished, God of abundance, and this will be an ongoing conversation between us. Each day I discover new gifts you offer me, and the list of reasons to be thankful grows. As I accept your gifts and live with them thankfully, guide me to become a person who shares with others so that they, too, can live abundantly.

May someone, somewhere, someday say of me, "I am thankful to have this person in my life."

January 30

> *In my distress I called upon the Lord,*
> *and cried to my God: and he did hear my*
> *voice out of his temple, and my cry did*
> *enter into his ears.*
>
> *−2 Samuel 22:7*

Lord, I want my thoughts to be like your thoughts. I want to discern what you discern and have the insight you have into all that happens in the world. I know that can never really be, Lord, but if I am open to your Spirit at all times, perhaps I can construe your hopes now and then. May my mind never be so cluttered that I fail to receive a message you are trying to share with me, Lord.

January 31

Whatever is right and pure,
excellent and gracious,
admirable and beautiful,
fill my mind with these things.

Too much of the world
comes to me in tones of gray and brown.
Too great the temptation
to indulge obsessive thoughts
and sordid plans.

Guard my mind;
place a fence around my motives.
The pure, the lovely, the good—
Yes! Only those today.

February

February 1

Winter has its beauty. There is a crystalline quality to the light, and at day's end, the horizon's blues and pinks take on a clarity peculiar to the season. Every tree, every building, becomes sharp-edged and gilded. We breathe in, and the cold fills our lungs; we are clear in our thoughts.

February 2

Wondrous God, I praise your name.
Your Word is life.
I believe you can heal me.
Be with me when I am sick, and remind me to praise
you when I am well.
Thank you for healing me in the past,
And for future healing.
Keep me in good health
That I might serve you
And praise your name.
Amen.

February 3

*Giving thanks always for all things
unto God and the Father in the name of
our Lord Jesus Christ.*

–Ephesians 5:20

Thank you, Lord, for the hobbies that I enjoy. How much joy I get out of these pleasures! Thank you for the chance to create, play, and enjoy. I am grateful for the people who share my hobby and who have become my friends. What a gift to share the joy of our pastimes together!

February 4

Is illness your will, Lord? I need answers, for I want you to help me heal. But if you send illness, how can I trust you to heal? Reassure me that you will work everything out eventually. And when that isn't possible, be with me as I suffer. Freed from fear I can get stronger as your healing energy flows through me, restoring me to my abundant life.

February 5

My guard is constant and vigilant, protecting me against the next episode of my humanness. I know to err is human, but why so often? Peace only comes, God of wholeness, through reassurance that with you, mistakes, errors—even disasters—can yield treasures. I am so grateful.

February 6

Heavenly Father, when you made the earth, you were satisfied with the job and pronounced it "good." Because I am your child, I find satisfaction in creating, too. I give you thanks, Father, for the gift of creativity. Help me never to discourage but to encourage the sparks of creativity in my children, so they can experience the pleasure of struggle and fulfillment in making something new. Only you can satisfy our longing souls by filling them with creative achievement.

February 7

Even in the face of struggles and difficulties, there is a higher order of goodness at work in our lives. We may not be able to physically detect it at all times, but our faith knows the truth, and the truth sets us free.

February 8

> *Lest thou shouldest ponder the path of life, her ways are moveable, that thou canst not know them.*
>
> *—Proverbs 5:6*

How easily, O God of eternity, for us to assume our time is like the grains of sand on an ocean beach— vast and endless. Remind us that each of our lives is limited like the sand in the hourglass. May what we do with that sand, play in it, work in it, build our relationships, whatever, be wise use of this precious gift of living.

February 9

We become discouraged when we try to live according to our own time clocks. We want what we want, and we want it this very minute. Then, when we don't get it, we sink in the quicksand of hopelessness and defeat. Only when we realize that God is at work in our lives will we begin to relax and let things happen in due season. Fruit will not ripen any faster because we demand it but will ripen in all its sweet splendor when it is ready in spite of our demands.

February 10

Time binds words, bones,
And those who work together.
Time bends meanings, mountain spines, and daylight.
Time braids our calamity and joy,
Melts together our many moods,
Strains them and serves up to God the resulting libation;
Sweet or sour—strong or weak.
Time will take us,
From this measured dimension
And deliver us to eternity.
Blessed are those who help along the way.

February 11

Each prayer is a message of faith in God. We are saying,
"I trust you; lead me. I believe in you; guide me. I need
you; show me." When we offer ourselves openly, he will
always answer.

February 12

> *For thou hast been a strength to the poor,*
> *a strength to the needy in his distress,*
> *a refuge from the storm,*
> *a shadow from the heat.*
>
> *—Isaiah 25:4*

Mental illness can be so devastating, Lord. Few understand the heartaches involved in diseases that carry no apparent physical scars. Be with those friends, neighbors, and family members who deal daily with difficult situations of which we are often unaware. Touch them with your special love, and let them know that they can lean on you, Lord. Ease their burdens, quell their sadness, and calm their desperation. Bring peace and healing to these households.

February 13

Our help is in the name of the Lord,
who made heaven and earth.

–Psalm 124:8

We often hesitate to extend help unless asked. We don't want to interfere or overstep our boundaries, or we are afraid that our behavior will be misinterpreted. But an opportunity to assist others is a rare gift, and if your actions come from the heart, you will never be misjudged.

February 14

In Valentine's Day, a day to say "I love you,"
we remember you, O God. We are able to
love only because you first loved us. You
taught us how to love you and each other—
our family and our neighbors.

We want our children to know your perfect
love, and we invite the fragrance of your love
to permeate our home.

Heavenly Father, you are the
author of love. Write your name
on our children's hearts, so they
may enjoy the wondrous gifts
you have prepared for those
who love you.

February 15

> *While we look not at the things which are*
> *seen, but at the things which are not seen: for*
> *the things which are seen are temporal; but*
> *the things which are not seen are eternal.*
>
> *–2 Corinthians 4:18*

God, you are invisible but not unseen. You reveal your-self in creation and demonstrate your kindness in a stranger's sincere smile. You are intangible but not unfelt. You caress our faces with the wind and embrace us in a friend's arms. We look for you and feel your presence. Amen.

February 16

Your family may be less than ideal, but they are your family. It was more than luck or biology that brought you together, and you'll need more than these to keep you together. Faith and forgiveness, kindness and cooperation, laughter and love—these will preserve the precious bonds between you.

February 17

A chart of my efforts to change traces a jagged course, Lord, like the lines on a heart-rate monitor. Reassure me that instead of measuring my failures, ups and downs mean simply that I am alive and ever-changing. Help me become consistent, but deliver me from flat lines.

February 18

Thank you, God, for the salesclerk who took an extra moment to be gracious, for the person who delivered my mail, and for the drivers who yielded to me without hesitation. I do not know their names, but they blessed me today with their hard work and positive attitudes.

February 19

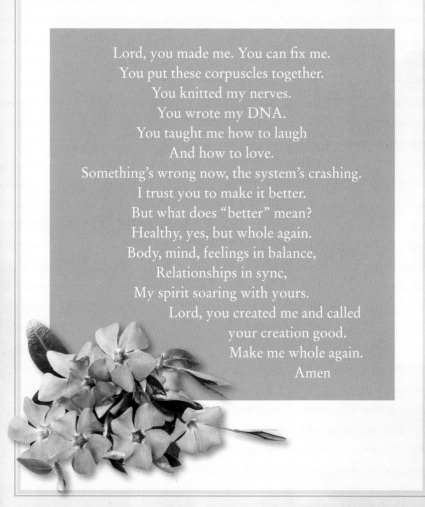

Lord, you made me. You can fix me.
You put these corpuscles together.
You knitted my nerves.
You wrote my DNA.
You taught me how to laugh
And how to love.
Something's wrong now, the system's crashing.
I trust you to make it better.
But what does "better" mean?
Healthy, yes, but whole again.
Body, mind, feelings in balance,
Relationships in sync,
My spirit soaring with yours.
Lord, you created me and called
your creation good.
Make me whole again.
Amen

February 20

Blessed are you who know how to celebrate the goodness of life.
Blessed because you choose to see the grace above and beyond the pain.
Blessed because you see a potential friend in every stranger you meet.
Blessed because you know the darkest clouds have brilliant silver linings.
And most blessed because: All you ever knew of the half-empty glass was that it was almost full.

February 21

Kindness is perhaps the most underrated and underused of all the virtues. People often don't have the time or energy for gestures of goodness and compassion. Yet the simple act of doing something for someone else is like a contagious epidemic that, when it spreads, threatens to bring about world peace.

February 22

Square by square, we live our lives marked off in neat appointment-calendar blocks of time. Everybody gets only so much, no more, for the lines are already bulging. We pencil in commitments that spill over into tomorrow's squares. And just look at yesterday's notations: Nowhere did we get every "to do" done, every deadline met. There is not enough time in the little squares we have allotted ourselves, O God, calling them life. We try using a larger calendar with bigger squares, but all we do is schedule heavier. Our pencils eat up our best intentions for accepting your promised abundant life. Help us, for we want to be more than just the sum of all we had scheduled, minus what we got done, multiplied by what we wished we'd been doing, tallying up to a bottom line of regret. Guide us as we erase what is not essential. Forgive us for the day-squares where we've inched you out; their hectic dreariness reflects your absence.

February 23

> *And Jesus came and spake unto them, saying, All power is given unto me in heaven and in earth. Go ye therefore, and teach all nations, baptizing them in the name of the Father, and of the Son, and of the Holy Ghost. Teaching them to observe all things whatsoever I have commanded you: and, lo, I am with you always, even unto the end of the world. Amen.*
>
> *–Matthew 28:18-20*

How we love a good story, O Divine Love. Especially a story with hope and promise and a good ending. When it comes to your Book, give me an open ear so that I might hear your good news, an open mind ready to accept it, and an open heart willing to be transformed by your love and acceptance of me.

February 24

> *But the Lord said unto Samuel,*
> *Look not on his countenance, or on the*
> *height of his stature; because I have refused*
> *him: for the Lord seeth not as man seeth;*
> *for man looketh on the outward appearance,*
> *but the Lord looketh on the heart.*
> *−1 Samuel 16:7*

This would be a great verse to hang over my bathroom mirror, Lord! As I work on my outward appearance each morning, help me to remember that my inner person needs attention too—especially since that's what you focus on. Your evaluation of my heart is far more important to me than any human opinion about my appearance or fashion sense.

February 25

God, we thank you for this food
for the hands that planted it
for the hands that tended it
for the hands that harvested it
for the hands that preprared it
for the hands that provided it
and for the hands that served it.
And we pray for those without enough food
in your world and in our land of plenty.

February 26

I can't make a blade of grass grow, Lord. By contrast, you created this entire universe and all it contains. If that doesn't inspire worship in my soul, I can't imagine what will. But the truth is that it does put me in awe of you; it does stir my heart to join in the worship of heaven.

February 27

Lord, today I ask you to slow me down and open my ears so I will notice the needs of those around me. Too often I breeze by people with an offhand greeting but remain in a cocoon of my own concerns. 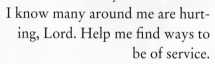 I know many around me are hurting, Lord. Help me find ways to be of service.

February 28

What we cannot do for ourselves, God can do for us. With our limited vision and perception, only God's wisdom can look beyond our lack and limitations. How comforting is it to know that we have this resource to turn to anytime we need? God is always ready to help us, to advise us, and to direct us.

February 29

There but for the grace of God go I.
God is my protection, and my guardian.
I know that I am always being watched over and
blessed because that is God's promise to me.
I walk in grace, and offer it to those
I meet along the way.
I stand in grace, letting it surround me with a love
that is eternal and forgiving of all my sins.

March

March 1

God, when life feels like a ride that won't let us off, remind us that you are waiting for us to reach up to you. And when we finally do, thank you for being there to lift us to peace and safety.

March 2

Bless you, Lord! The heavens declare your glory; the skies proclaim your mighty power. And here I am, looking up into those vast regions, knowing that the tiniest cell in my body is a most glorious miracle, as well. Bless you, Lord!

March 3

When we fill our days with the noisy blur of constant activity, we miss the gifts and blessings of silence and stillness. Only by purposely taking the time to do nothing can we cultivate the inner wisdom and guidance we seek. It's in the quiet that we renew our connection to the source of inspiration, energy, and enthusiasm. Silence is more than golden. It's essential to a life well-lived.

March 4

O Lord, if you don't remember our sins, why do we so often beat ourselves up over them? The only possible benefit I can see is that this way, there's less chance that we'll repeat them. But if it be your will, Lord—and to our benefit—grant us your sweet forgetfulness. We accept your gift of forgiveness, Lord. May we learn to accept your gift of forgetfulness as well.

March 5

Love makes us greater
than we ever were before,
takes what we have to give
and gives back even more.

Love makes us stronger
than we ever thought we'd be,
takes the load we have to bear
and sets our spirits free.

March 6

Lord, a vexing situation has me very confused. Is it possible I'm trying to sort it out through my own limited understanding and overlooking a crucial element? I know I can trust you with anything. I give this up to you and ask you to restore me to a place where I can look at what's going on in the right way— your way.

March 7

When I was a child, I had my favorite blanket. I took that blanket everywhere, wrapping myself in its warmth and comfort. Now I am all grown up, and you, God, are the one I turn to for that warmth and comfort. Like that blanket, I know all I have to do is call you and you will wrap your love around me and make me feel safe and snug. I am your child still, and no matter how old I get, I will always need you watching over me and making sure I am happy and secure. For you, God, are my permanent security blanket, my safe harbor from the storm, my rock, my home.

March 8

Casting all your care upon him;
for he careth for you.

—1 Peter 5:7

Lord, as we move through this Lenten season, let me not be afraid of the wilderness. Let me not be afraid of unanswered questions, of uncertain paths, of scarcity. Let me trust in you and your lovingkindness, that I will have what I need when I need it. Let me trust in your "daily bread," and not get wound up in worries about the future.

March 9

Lord, we live in a world where there is a great clamoring for power and glory. Greed runs rampant, and time and again we see the inglorious results of someone's unethical attempts to climb to the top. Protect us from such fruitless ambition, Lord. For we know that it is only when we humble ourselves that you will lift us up higher than we could ever have imagined. All power and glory is yours, forever and ever. Until we acknowledge that truth, we will never be great in anyone's eyes—especially yours.

March 10

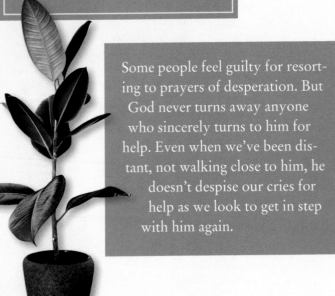

> *Then they cried unto the Lord in their trouble, and he delivered them out of their distresses.*
>
> *—Psalm 107:6*

Some people feel guilty for resorting to prayers of desperation. But God never turns away anyone who sincerely turns to him for help. Even when we've been distant, not walking close to him, he doesn't despise our cries for help as we look to get in step with him again.

March 11

Have you ever met someone who solely defines themselves by their possessions? Though society may seem to reward those who achieve their self-worth from having the "right" car, or the biggest house, these individuals are, at the root of it, unhappy people. Material gain in and of itself is, ultimately, an empty victory. Don't be that person. Don't let your worldly interests cloud your true sense of self.

Dear God, may what really matters define who I am as a person!

March 12

Lord, you are my lighthouse,
shining like a beacon
in a raging storm,
guiding my way
through the fog and rough seas.
I set my course on you
with patience, perseverance,
and faith, trusting
that you will help me
reach calmer shores.

March 13

This month brings the first inklings of spring to my area, though the trees are still bare. But that seems appropriate, during this month that takes place during the season of Lent. Lord, this month, empty my heart of distractions. Walk with me to the desert and stay with me there, as you pare away those things that draw me away from you.

March 14

I will cry unto God most high;
unto God that performeth all things for me.

—Psalm 57:2

Lord, although we are often not certain
of your intentions when you present us
with unpleasant circumstances, we
understand that you do have a reason. The hurt isn't just to spite us.
Please help us to keep our out-
looks positive and allow us to
aid others who are as dismayed
and in just as much pain as we
are. Amen.

March 15

> *Greater love hath no man than this,*
> *that a man lay down his life for his friends.*
>
> *–John 15:13*

I thank you for the healing power of friends and for the positive emotions friendship brings. Thank you for sending companions to me so we can support and encourage one another and share our joys and sorrows. My friends represent for me your presence and friendship here on earth. Please keep them in your care, Father. We need each other, and we need you. Amen.

March 16

The mind is like a garden of fertile soil into which the seeds of our thoughts, ideas, and intentions are planted. With loving care and nurturing attention, those seeds bloom forth to manifest in our lives as wonderful opportunities and events. Those seeds that we choose to either ignore or neglect will simply die off. Thus, our mind constantly turns over old growth into new. It is where we focus our energy and give our love that breaks through the dark soil into the light of day. It then becomes the visible good in our life, casting off new seeds to one day bloom forth in a cycle of renewal and abundance.

March 17

Wondrous God, I praise your name.
Your Word is life.
I believe you can heal me.
Be with me when I am sick, and remind me to praise
you when I am well.
Thank you for healing me in the past,
And for future healing.
Keep me in good health
That I might serve you
And praise your name.
Amen.

March 18

Have not I commanded thee?
Be strong and of a good courage;
be not afraid, neither be thou dismayed:
for the Lord thy God is with thee
whithersoever thou goest.

–Joshua 1:9

We wander like children lost in a cave, perilously close to the edge of despair. Unable to see where we're going, we crouch in fear rather than risk falling while searching for an exit. Nudge us beyond fear; send us guides who have traveled dark passages before.

March 19

Now there are diversities of gifts, but the same Spirit. And there are differences of administrations, but the same Lord. And there are diversities of operations, but it is the same God which worketh all in all.

–1 Corinthians 12:4-6

Every person has a special gift. One may be a computer whiz; another may have the gift of being a gracious host. Respect the gifts of others as you wish to be respected for your gifts.

March 20

And be ye kind one to another,
tenderhearted, forgiving one another,
even as God for Christ's sake
hath forgiven you.

–Ephesians 4:32

When trouble strikes, we're restored by the smallest
gestures from God's ambassadors: friends, random kindnesses, shared pain and support, even a stranger's out-
stretched hand. And we get the message: God cares.

March 21

Spring is the season of moving—the real estate market picks up, and "for sale" signs crop up in the neighborhood. Please bless all who are preparing for moves, that they find a house that can be a true home. Please bless those who are not moving by choice—those who are relocating for a spouse's job, or no longer able to maintain their home because of age. Please help us all remember that you go with us everywhere, and that we do not need to fear change when you are with us.

March 22

> *Be not forgetful to entertain strangers:*
> *for thereby some have*
> *entertained angels unawares.*
>
> *—Hebrews 13:2*

Why are we surprised that we are not alone? Sound
waves swim around our heads each moment, but
until we tune them in, we never hear the message.
In the same way, angels swarm our lives every day,
but unless we remember how to listen, we are never
aware of their presence.

March 23

> *Therefore if any man be in Christ, he is a new creature: old things are passed away; behold, all things are become new.*
>
> *–2 Corinthians 5:17*

Here we are again, Lord. Another time when I feel like I've made a complete mess of this life you've given me. I place myself in your hands. If you need to totally reshape me to turn me into someone more useful, so be it! Thank you for not abandoning me, your humble creation. Make me over in your design.

March 24

Enliven my imagination, God of new life, so that I can see through to-day's troubles to coming newness. Surround me with your caring so that I can live as if the new has already begun.

March 25

You call me to courage, Lord, but incrementally, as a child emboldened to walk along placing each small foot in larger footprints. Following father or mother—as I am following you—knowing a path marked out this way—just step by step—but you can only lead to safety.

March 26

My Creator, blessed is your presence. For you and you alone give me power to walk through dark valleys into the light again. You and you alone give me hope when there seems no end to my suffering. You and you alone give me peace when the noise of my life overwhelms me. I ask that you give this same power, hope, and peace to all who know discouragement, that they, too, may be emboldened and renewed by your everlasting love. Amen.

March 27

Be not overcome of evil,
but overcome evil with good.

–Romans 12:21

God, teach me to have the courage to act in the world as you wish me to. Help me find a way to push through the challenges that arise in my path, and show me how to overcome evil with love and compassion. Help me to stand tall against fear and stay in the light. Amen.

March 28

> *Teach me to do thy will;*
> *for thou art my God: thy spirit is good;*
> *lead me into the land of uprightness.*
>
> *—Psalm 143:10*

Life goes back and forth between push and pull, force and acceptance, fight and surrender. It's exhausting! But staying in God's will makes the doors of life open easier and more frequently than when we rely only on ourselves.

March 29

When we think of integrity, we think of someone who is honorable and trustworthy—a person who keeps their word and guards their reputation. To be called a man or woman of integrity is a high compliment. Such a person knows the difference between right and wrong and diligently pursues doing right, no matter what the obstacles. Jesus provides the best example of a man of integrity; he was not swayed by outer influences but lived a life above reproach. Integrity comes not just from the pursuit of right living, but the pursuit of God, which leads to right living.

March 30

Dear God,

As I rise each day, give me the strength, courage, and patience to do the best I can for my family. All through the day, guide me with your grace and divine direction into right action and right decision. And when the day is done and it is time for me to rest my weary mind and body, take the burden of my troubles from me so that I can sleep. Watch over me and mine throughout the night, and when it is time to arise to a new day, be there for me all over again. Amen.

March 31

And whatsoever ye do in word or deed, do all in the name of the Lord Jesus, giving thanks to God and the Father by him.

—Colossians 3:17

Gratitude may be the most highly underestimated virtue. We think of love, hope, faith and the power of prayer and forgiveness. But how often do we stop each day and give thanks for all the blessings in our lives? Are we too focused on what we lack, what we don't have, don't want, don't need? By opening the heart and mind to focus on gratitude, we unleash a treasure of unceasing good that's just waiting to overflow into our lives. A grateful person knows that by giving thanks, they're given even more to be thankful for.

April

April 1

A friend is one who understands
Any loss or gain.
A friend is one who knows your thoughts,
And whose feelings will remain.
A friend is one who encourages you,
And supports all your decisions,
A friend is one who yearns with you,
And can see your grandest visions.
A friend is one who helps you through,
Those long and stressful days.
A friend is one who lifts you up,
In a hundred different ways.
A friend is one who loves you much,
Just the way you are.
A friend is one who's in your heart,
Whether near to you or far.

April 2

Father, it stings when the ones I love correct me. I don't like to be wrong or feel like I'm being criticized. But that's just wounded pride revealing itself. Deep down I appreciate learning the truth so I can learn and grow. Flattery feels nice in the moment, but it doesn't do much real good. People who risk hurting me because they love me are the ones I should listen to. Help me get over my wounded pride quickly and move on in light of what I've learned. And bless those who care enough for me to speak the truth in love.

April 3

It takes great courage to heal, Lord,
great energy to reach out from
this darkness to touch the hem
of your garment and ask
for healing. Bless the brave
voices telling nightmare
tales of dreadful wounds
to the gifted heal-
ers of this world.
Together, sufferers
and healers are binding
up damaged parts
and laying down
burdens carried
so long.

April 4

For God so loved the world,
that he gave his only begotten son,
that whosoever believeth in him should not
perish, but have everlasting life.

–John 3:16

Dear Father God, you sent your son to us to be our Lord, to watch over us, to bring us comfort, strength, hope, and healing when our hearts are broken and our lives seem shattered. We will never be alone, not when you are here with us always and forever. Remind us to look to you for strength. Amen.

April 5

Help me, God, to see that you gave your love in such a way that even the most wicked person can repent and find new life in your grace and mercy; indeed, that your love calls even the worst sinners to become your children. You created each person with a specific purpose to serve in this world. Help me, Lord, to pray that each person will turn away from evil, turn to you, and become your devoted servant. Amen.

April 6

A kind act by a stranger is a wonderful surprise! I don't expect someone to let me go ahead in line at the store or to return an item I had lost. What a blessing it is when people reach out to others. Thank you for the small acts that make my day better, and thank you for the opportunity to be a blessing to others by finding small ways to make their day brighter.

April 7

Lord, you are my lighthouse,
shining like a beacon
in a raging storm,
guiding my way
through the fog and rough seas.

I set my course on you
with patience, perseverance,
and faith, trusting
that you will help me
reach calmer shores.

April 8

Time helps, Lord, but it never quite blunts the loneliness that loss brings. Thank you for the peace that is slowly seeping into my pores, allowing me to live with the unlivable; to bear the unbearable.

Guide and bless my faltering steps down a new road. Prop me up when I think I can't go it alone; prod me when I tarry too long in lonely self-pity.

Most of all, Kind Healer, thank you for the gifts of memory and dreams. The one comforts, the other beckons, both halves of a healing whole.

April 9

Jesus fulfilled many roles during his earthly life: son, friend, teacher, and savior. He grappled with many issues—just as we do—but he patiently fulfilled the mission he came to earth to perform. When family friends ran out of wine at the wedding at Cana, Jesus' mother asked him to do something. Jesus hesitated for a moment because he wasn't sure it was time for him to draw such attention to himself, but he soon acquiesced, realizing that his time had, indeed, come. May we follow Jesus' example and always be open to your plans for our lives, Lord.

April 10

*So then faith cometh
by hearing, and hearing by
the word of God.*

–Romans 10:17

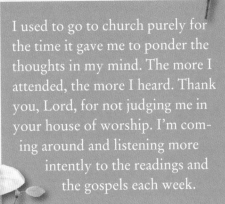

I used to go to church purely for the time it gave me to ponder the thoughts in my mind. The more I attended, the more I heard. Thank you, Lord, for not judging me in your house of worship. I'm coming around and listening more intently to the readings and the gospels each week.

April 11

Lord, it's hard to wait for word about my new job. Did I get it? Did they turn me down? I'm so looking forward to starting, so why the delay? Can't they make up their minds?

Yes, I do need patience more than anything else—and right now! Please quell my anger and help me see that if this isn't the right place for me, I can trust you to keep it from me. But it's hard to wait. Still hard to wait.

April 12

Be careful for nothing; but in every thing by prayer and supplication with thanksgiving let your requests be made known unto God. And the peace of God, which passeth all understanding, shall keep your hearts and minds through Christ Jesus.

–Philippians 4:6-7

Lord, even though I know worry is a useless waste of time and energy, it snares me again and again. Thank you for helping me notice early on that I'm about to wallow in worry once more. As I give this situation to you, Lord, I release my need to worry about it as well. Instead, I look for the blessings in the midst of all that's going on and thank you wholeheartedly for them. I willingly trade my worry for your peace.

God has shown what he requires:
To do what's right,
to love what's kind,
To walk humble-hearted
With him.
But, inside, my secret heart desires
To do as inclined,
To love what's mine,
To walk self-centered,
Alone.
Good conscience, please
inquire:
What shall I do this time?
Which love's first in line?
Where shall I walk?
Beside.

April 14

Lord, we've tossed our prayers aloft, and hopefully, expectantly, we wait for your answers. As we do, we will: listen, for you speak in the voice of nature; see you as a companion in the face and hand of a friend; feel you as a sweet-smelling rain, a river breeze; believe you can provide encouragement, direction, and guidance for those who have only to ask. We feel your presence.

April 15

May you be the leader you were meant to be today. May you find courage to temper your business goals with an eye toward human compassion. May you carefully weigh the consequences of every tough decision you make—the effects on the company and the impact on all who work within it. May you know that one greater than you goes before you and stands behind you, offering great wisdom. And in this knowledge may you seek to lead just as he did: being servant of all.

April 16

> *I thank God,*
> *whom I serve from my forefathers*
> *with pure conscience,*
> *that without ceasing I have*
> *remembrance of thee in my prayers*
> *night and day.*
>
> *–2 Timothy 1:3*

Lord, being in love is a gift. Everything seems brighter and sharper in focus. My heart soars and my spirit is light as air, and all because of the love of another. But help me to also seek that deeper, more lasting love that comes from truly knowing another, even when the fires of passion become a gentle and steady simmer. Let love always be in my life, no matter what form it comes in. Love of any kind is a gift. Thank you, Lord.

April 17

O Holy Creator, who hath bound together heaven and earth, let me walk through your kingdom comforted and protected by the warm rays of your love. Let me be healed as I stand basking in the divine light of your presence, where strength and hope and joy are found. Let me sit at rest in the valley of your peace, surrounded by the fortress of your loving care.

April 18

Rejoice when I run into problems?
Know trials are good for me?
Things like that aren't easy—
Learning to live patiently.

Growing in grace is a process.
Developing character hurts.
Becoming more Christ-like in all things
Is an everyday process called work.

But if I have faith it is possible.
Faith knowing God loves and cares—
That all my burdens and trials
He also feels and shares.

April 19

Time is one commodity that we can invest in for the future with guaranteed high returns. In fact, the more energy, enthusiasm, and creativity we put into the time we've been given, the more we'll get back in the form of new experiences and opportunities for a successful and prosperous life. Time well spent is the best investment we can ever make, and it doesn't cost a thing.

April 20

Among the proliferation of bumper-sticker slogans, statements and sentiments, there's one sticker that encourages people to "practice random acts of kindness." It's a great little reminder. For whenever we make a conscious effort to be kind to others—especially to those whom we usually tend to avoid, overlook, or ignore—we take the first step toward seeing them as God sees them: through the eyes of love.

April 21

Lord, this is one of those
days when I really don't
know which way to turn. I've
lost my sense of direction and feel as
if I'm sitting on a rock in the forest,
wondering which trail will take
me back to familiar ground. Lead me,
Lord. Send the signs I need to follow
to get where you want me to go. I
put my trust in you.

April 22

Friends come and go, but God remains. Life is filled with relationships between friends, family, and loved ones. Some of those will last a season or two, some may last forever. But the one true friendship we will never lose is the one we have with God. The presence of God does not come and go like the tides of the ocean. The presence of God is forever.

April 23

> *But by the grace of God I am what I am: and his grace which was bestowed upon me was not in vain; but I laboured more abundantly than they all: yet not I, but the grace of God which was with me.*
>
> *—1 Corinthians 15:10*

There but for the grace of God go I. God is my protection, and my guardian. I know that I am always being watched over and blessed because that is God's promise to me. I walk in grace, and offer it to those I meet along the way. I stand in grace, letting it surround me with a love that is eternal and forgiving of all my sins.

April 24

Too often we lie
when people say,
How are you?
We say, "I'm fine."
We smile, and put
on our happy face.

Why can't we be honest,
at least with loved ones,
and say, "I hurt"?

Why can't we cry honest tears
and let a friend
comfort us for a moment—
embrace us
with loving arms,
as we take off
the mask we wear
to hide the pain?

April 25

Opposites don't attract nearly as often as they repel, if we are to believe the headlines. Pick a race, color, creed, or lifestyle, Lord of all, and we'll find something to fight about. Deliver us from stereotypes. Inspire us to spot value in everyone we meet. As we dodge the curses and hatred, we are relieved there is room for all of us beneath your wings. Bless our diversity; may it flourish.

April 26

From personal experience, I think "spilling the beans" sounds too harmless to describe gossip, Lord. I've had so-called "spilled beans" tarnish my reputation, harm relationships, and expose parts of my soul I wanted kept private. But the bright side is that I've learned the importance of finding trustworthy confidants—and of being one. Still, there are times when I'm tempted to talk when I shouldn't or am careless with my "thinking out loud." Help me guard the dignity of those who have confided in me by keeping quiet or speaking only when, how, and where I should.

April 27

> *For the Son of Man is come to seek and to save that which was lost.*
>
> *—Luke 19:10*

You never have to walk alone through life, because God walks with you. Whether your path is smooth and free of obstacles, or rough and filled with detours, God is there to help guide you and give you the strength to carry on and keep moving forward. There is no reason to feel lonely, and there is nothing to fear. God is there, now and always.

April 28

No matter what mistakes you have made, God is ready to show favor upon you. No matter how much you have messed up your life, God is ready with love and understanding to help you reclaim what was lost. No matter how sad or depressed you may be feeling, God is ready to wrap you in arms of loving grace and make you feel cared for again.

April 29

Have you ever felt the power of God's amazing grace? Have you ever tasted the sweetness of God's merciful forgiveness? Have you ever heard God's kind words of understanding and support? You will know it when you do, for all darkness will be made light, and all suffering will give way to a new joyfulness and inner peace. This is the power of God's amazing grace.

April 30

I appreciate the connections made possible by social media, but I also recognize that like everything else, when it comes to technology, moderation is key. Yesterday I was glued to a series of screens throughout the day, from phone to laptop, and when I tore myself away to make dinner, I found myself in a particularly ill humor. While I had happily corresponded with an old friend who lives on another continent, I'd also witnessed a good deal of negativity, judgmental attitudes, and blatantly hateful behavior online. The prolonged exposure had soured my spirit, and when I snapped at my son, I realized that my choices that day did not benefit my family or me. God, help me to capitalize on the good inherent in technology, while also practicing moderation and sound judgment. Do not let me fall prey to the negativity that can be part of the online experience.

May

May 1

If we live in the Spirit,
let us also walk in the Spirit.

–Galatians 5:25

It's hard, Lord, to reveal my heart to you, though
it's the thing I most want to do. Remind me in this
dialogue that you already know what is within me.
You wait—O thank you! —hoping for the gift of my
willingness to acknowledge the good you already see
and the bad you've long forgotten.

May 2

Without suffering, there would be no learning.
Without learning, there would be no wisdom.
Without wisdom, there would be no understanding.
Without understanding, there would be no acceptance.
Without acceptance, there would be no forgiveness.
Without forgiveness there would be no joy.
Without joy, there would be no love.
Without love, there would be no life.

May 3

God, thank you for sometimes reminding me that in the center of chaos lies the seed of new opportunity and that things are not always as awful as they seem at first. I often forget that what starts out bad can end up great and that it is all a matter of my own perspective. Amen.

May 4

He sent redemption unto his people:
he hath commanded his covenant
for ever: holy and reverend is
his name.

–Psalm 111:9

When it seems that scarcely a day ends by saying, "If only I could do it over. I regret what I said, did, or didn't do," the God of fresh starts is eager to make things right. All you need to say is, "Forgive me for today, and show me how to redeem myself for tomorrow."

May 5

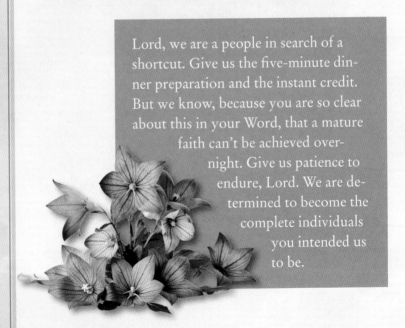

Lord, we are a people in search of a shortcut. Give us the five-minute dinner preparation and the instant credit. But we know, because you are so clear about this in your Word, that a mature faith can't be achieved overnight. Give us patience to endure, Lord. We are determined to become the complete individuals you intended us to be.

May 6

> *O give thanks unto the Lord, for he is good: for his mercy endureth for ever.*
>
> *—Proverbs 10:12*

Thank you, God, for my five senses. I am grateful for being able to see, hear, taste, touch, and smell. How wonderful to see nature's beauty, to hear the voices of my loved ones, to taste good food, to smell the fresh scent of spring, and to touch a loved one's skin. My senses let me experience the world, and I give thanks for that gift today.

May 7

The alarm goes off; you can smell coffee perking. Your mind leaps to action, already making lists of priorities for the day. But before you ratchet to high gear, try this: stop. Just for five minutes. Lie in bed and just . . . breathe. You don't have to close your eyes (you might fall back to sleep!); can you see the sky outside your window? Watch a cloud. Feel your breath. Five minutes, that's all; a new day waits.

May 8

When sorrow comes to us, it can be overwhelming. We feel unable to move and incapable of the patience necessary to wait for the healing that will come with time. Knowing you are there, Lord, brings the most comfort.

It is even harder to watch a loved one grieve. We feel left outside with no way to reach in and bring comfort. Words fail. Kind gestures fall short. But when we remember that what comforts us most is your presence, we know what to do: just be there—listening, praying, and loving—allowing your Spirit to pervade the space around us.

May 9

Lord, how we want to run to you in times of need—
and how blessed we are that we always find you
available. You always take us in and calm our weary
spirits. You, O Lord, are mighty and unchangeable!
At times when everything seems shaky and uncertain,
you are firm and immovable. We praise you, Lord!

May 10

What a gift friendship is! I am grateful for my friends. Some friends have known me for many years. We grew up together and watched each other change and grow. Other friends are newer, but no less dear. Thank you, Lord, for all the friends you have placed in my life and for the memories we have created together.

May 11

Life can be complicated; in the larger world we are challenged, sometimes on a daily basis, to be our best selves. Perhaps we don't see eye-to-eye with a co-worker. Maybe we need to have a talk with a friend who has hurt us, even though we dislike confrontation. Can it be that the sweet, adoring toddler we walked to preschool seemingly yesterday has morphed into a teen who is trying to individuate—but doesn't yet know how to do that in a mature or loving way? Though life's hurts can chip away at our spirits, God reminds us that each of us has value. May we never lose sight of the fact that God created us! May we never lose sight of our inherent worth.

May 12

> *I have shewed you all things,*
> *how that so labouring ye ought to support*
> *the weak, and to remember the words*
> *of the Lord Jesus, how he said, It is more*
> *blessed to give than to receive.*
>
> *—Acts 20:35*

We all have something to offer: time, money, expertise. God exhorts us to give generously; in his infinite wisdom, he understands that when we give, we're not just helping others (worthy in and of itself). But we also help ourselves. Studies have shown that generosity helps to manage personal stress, and have linked unselfishness and giving with a general sense of life satisfaction and a lower risk of early death. When we reach outside ourselves, we connect with others; God wants that connection, that sense of purpose and happiness, for each of us. Dear Lord, help us to connect with our best selves; help us to be generous givers.

May 13

God, when I feel unsteady, you alone provide the firm ground beneath my feet. Illuminate my path so that I am always living in your will and not from my own limited ego. Show me how to be the best I can be under all circumstances, good and bad.

Father, I pray today for a clear path, a strong wind at my back pushing me forward, and the courage of a lion to step into greatness. I am afraid and uncomfortable, but with you I can begin the journey of a thousand miles—with one bold step.

May 15

Lord, sometimes I resist your grace. It's not that I don't want to be closer to you, but I know I don't deserve it. I stew over my past sins, wallowing in guilt. I don't want to take your forgiveness for granted, but neither do I want to forget that you are always reaching out to me, ready to draw me back to you.

May 16

I exhort therefore, that, first of all,
supplications, prayers, intercessions,
and giving of thanks, be made for all men.

—1 Timothy 2:1

Who shall I pray for today, Lord? I don't want to pray only for my needs and my wants, but to hold others up to you in prayer. Please bring to my mind the names of those who most need prayer today.

May 17

> *But he was wounded for our transgressions,*
> *he was bruised for our iniquities:*
> *the chastisement of our peace was upon him;*
> *and with his stripes we are healed.*
>
> *—Isaiah 53:5*

Father God, you gave a staggering gift through your son, Jesus Christ. How can I express my gratitude for the gift of salvation? Sometimes I need to sit in silence, surrounded by your presence, as I reflect on your love for me.

May 18

It's not hard to love
those who sparkle—
the diamond people
in the world.
The real test of loving
is being able to love
those who are like
pieces of coal—
those diamonds
in the rough
who might get us dirty.
But if we love them
even so—
with enough positive pressure
from love,
one day
they'll be diamonds too!

May 19

> *Forbearing one another,*
> *and forgiving one another, if any man*
> *have a quarrel against any:*
> *even as Christ forgave you, so also*
> *do ye.*
>
> —Colossians 3:13

I pray, Lord, for the ability to learn forgiveness. Often within my heart there is much that is negative. I pray to learn to let go of those feelings. I pray to learn to forgive others as I wish to be forgiven. I pray for the gifts of understanding and compassion as I strive to be more like you. Amen.

May 20

> *Peace I leave with you,*
> *my peace I give unto you: not as the*
> *world giveth, give I unto you.*
> *Let not your heart be troubled,*
> *neither let it be afraid.*
>
> *–John 14:27*

What is peace? Is it the absence of conflict, or the ability to stay calm and centered in God's love during the most trying of times? Peace is not something we only find at the end of a long battle. It is always available when we come to understand that with God on our side, there is never a battle to begin with.

May 21

Father in heaven, when all else fails, I turn to you for the comfort only you can provide. I have done all I can do, and now I rest in the belief that you are taking from me my burdens and doing for me what I cannot. In you alone do I find that comforting assurance that everything is being taken care of and that all will work out as it should. My surrender to your comfort is not out of weakness but out of my faith in your eternal love and concern for me. For that I am grateful.

May 22

> *How great are his signs and how mighty are his wonders! His kingdom is an everlasting kingdom, and his dominion is from generation to generation.*
>
> *– Daniel 4:3*

Show me a sign, dear God, to help me figure out this problem I am struggling with. Give me something my spirit will recognize to help me overcome what stands in the way of my happiness. Help me, God, to see your solution as the calm within the storm.

May 23

Here is a place you can stop and rest for a while.
Here is a place you can lay down your worries and let
go of the weight of your fears upon your shoulders.
Here is a place you can breathe deeply of fresh air,
and feel the warmth of the sun on your skin. Here is a
place filled with tranquility, like a beautiful garden.
Here is where you are, with God.

May 24

> *Great is our Lord,*
> *and of great power:*
> *his understanding is infinite.*
>
> *—Psalm 147:5*

God knows of your suffering and your troubles. God knows of your sorrow and your pain. God knows you seek peace from the turmoil of life and offers you his loving presence. It costs you nothing but the willingness to accept it. It is always available, day or night, just for the asking. When life grows difficult, God's peace washes over you like a gentle and comforting rain.

May 25

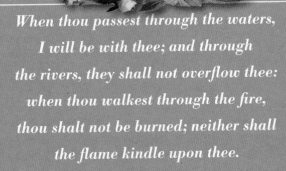

Living with stress causes so many health problems, not to mention strain on your mental and emotional state. Perhaps you cannot remove everything in life that causes you stress, but you can approach it with a sense of inner peace that makes you unshakeable and unstoppable. Life will never be perfectly calm, but as long as you are within, where God lives and moves and has his being, it won't matter what is happening on the outside.

May 26

God, I feel happy today, and I have you to thank for that. No matter what is going on outside of me, I am strong and safe and secure inside because you love and care for me. Thank you for loving me when I have been cranky, tired, lazy, and even mean. Thank you for being there when I ignored your presence, God. Your steadfast love is a constant reminder of just how good I have it in life. And that makes me happiest of all!

May 27

Hope is an anchor to the soul. It can keep us from drifting aimlessly, getting caught in whirlpools, or running into sandbars. This anchor is essential in a world so full of various waves. Sometimes those waves slap us from behind; sometimes we see them coming but cannot get out of the way. In all cases, hope ties us to safety. The waves come and go in their fury or playfulness—but hope is always there.

May 28

One song can spark a moment,
One flower can wake the dream.
One tree can start a forest,
One bird can herald spring.
One smile begins a friendship,
One hand clasp lifts a soul.
One star can guide a ship at sea,
One word can frame the goal.
One vote can change a nation,
One sunbeam lights a room.
One candle wipes out darkness,
One laugh will conquer gloom.

May 29

O God of rest and rejuvenation, guide me to find ways to let your nurturing reach me. I need to be healthy and well-rested in order to provide, lead, and inspire. Burning the candle at both ends all the time is hardly an example I'm proud of.

May 30

And it shall come to pass afterward,
that I will pour out my spirit upon all flesh;
and your sons and your daughters shall
prophesy, your old men shall dream dreams,
your young men shall see visions.

–Joel 2:28

I always want to be a dreamer, O God, to feel the stir and the yearning to see my vision become reality. There are those who would say dreamers are free-floaters. When I dream I feel connected to you and to your creation, bound by purpose and a sense of call. Nourish my dreams and my striving to make them real.

May 31

Lord, you have told us to "remember the days of old." Memorials have played a large part in the history of your people in Israel, and we thank you for these reminders to honor the past.

As we remember those who have gone before us, we teach our children love and respect for life itself.

In giving honor to others, we thank and honor you, O God, for your love and for the great sacrifice of your son, Jesus Christ.

June

June 1

It's easy to love a friend for all the things we have in common. It's harder, but much more valuable, to love the things that set us apart from one another. Learning to appreciate our differences brings a new level of intimacy to our relationships with others.

June 2

Sometimes we believe our souls can only be at peace if there is no outer turmoil. The wonder of God's peace is that even when the world around us is in confusion and our emotions are in a whirl, underneath it all we can know his peace.

June 3

Please let me help you
however I can.
Long ages ago
it was God's plan
for me to serve,
to love and to share—
helping ease another's
burden of care.
So let me be
God's loving gift to you
because in serving others,
I am blessed, too.

June 4

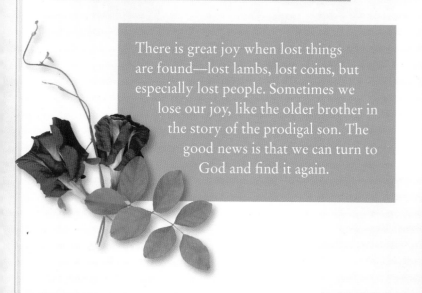

*It was meet that we should
make merry, and be glad:
for this thy brother was dead,
and is alive again; and was lost,
and is found.*

–Luke 15:32

There is great joy when lost things
are found—lost lambs, lost coins, but
especially lost people. Sometimes we
lose our joy, like the older brother in
the story of the prodigal son. The
good news is that we can turn to
God and find it again.

June 5

The light that shines upon me,
The arms that reach to hold me,
The warmth that gives me comfort,
The angel's wings enfold me.

The word that gives me power,
The song that makes me whole,
The wisdom that empowers me,
The touch that heals my soul.

June 6

Heavenly Father, teach me to forgive others their transgressions and to let go of angers and resentments that poison the heart and burden the soul. Teach me to love and understand others and to accept them as they are, not as I wish they would be. Amen.

June 7

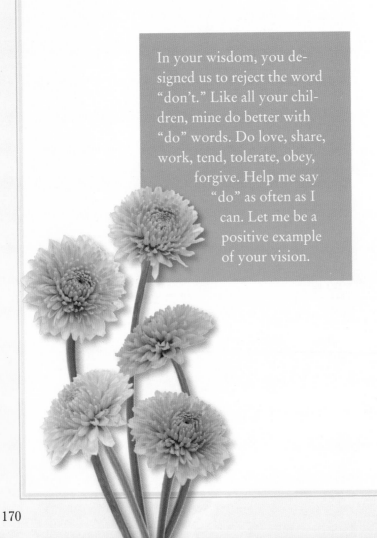

In your wisdom, you designed us to reject the word "don't." Like all your children, mine do better with "do" words. Do love, share, work, tend, tolerate, obey, forgive. Help me say "do" as often as I can. Let me be a positive example of your vision.

June 8

*Let no corrupt communication
proceed out of your mouth,
but that which is good to the
use of edifying, that it may
minister grace unto the hearers.*

—Ephesians 4:29

Bless me with a peacemaker's kind
heart and a builder's sturdy hand, Lord,
for these are mean-spirited, litigious
times when we tear down with words and
weapons first and ask questions later. Help
me take every opportunity to compliment,
praise, and applaud as I rebuild peace.

June 9

For his eyes are upon the ways of man,
and he seeth all his goings.

–Job 34:21

You are everywhere, Lord, and we're comforted to be
enfolded as we move through life's extremes. You are
with us in birthings and dyings, in routine and surprise, and in stillness and activity. We cannot wander
so far in any direction that you are not already there.

June 10

Bless my attempts at success, Lord, though
I know many of them will end in failure.
I pray that you will even bless my failures, for I also know that never risking
is a sure sign of sloth and a ques-
tioning of your constant goodwill
toward me.

June 11

O Lord, what a blessing children are in this world. They bring such joy into our lives and are a precious composite of the best of our past and the hopes for the future. Thank you for your love for all children, Lord. Please guard them always.

June 12

> *Yea, though I walk through the valley of the shadow of death,*
> *I will fear no evil: for thou art with me; thy rod and thy staff they comfort me.*
>
> —*Psalm 23:4*

Many times I feel that I have the right to be downcast. But God's Word says that we should not be downcast because we have an amazing hope through him. If I focus on this hope, joy will enter my spirit, and my negative emotions will disperse.

June 13

Heavenly Father, your son, Jesus, could have called down heaven to destroy his enemies when he was on earth, but he didn't. Revenge wasn't his mission. Love was. Help me to submit, as he did, to a path of gentleness in the strength of your love. Amen.

June 14

Lord, you're never missing in action—
you're with me all the time, everywhere,
without fail. Please keep this knowledge
in the forefront of my mind today so I'll
be encouraged and emboldened to move
through each challenge without feeling
intimidated, fearful, or ashamed. May
I always be kept safe because of
your keeping power
at work in my life. In
your name, I pray.

June 15

Beloved, if God so loved us,
we ought also to love one another.

—1 John 4:11

To love one is to love all, for in truth we are all one. To know one is to know all, for in truth we are all the same inside. To help one is to help all, for in truth we are all interdependent. To give to one is to give to all, for in truth we are all connected.

June 16

The God who hung the stars in space will turn
   your darkness into light.
The God whose birds rise on the winds will give
   your injured soul new flight.
The God who taught the whale its song will
   cause your heart to sing again.
For the God whose power made earth and sky
   will touch you with his gentle hand.

June 17

May you be healed, in mind, body, and soul. May you come to know that all healing proceeds from God, and he cares about every part of you. Perhaps the healing will come sooner for your attitude than for your body. Perhaps your mind will experience peace quicker than bones and muscles. But sooner or later, all will be well.

June 18

Though you may stumble and fall along the way, God will be at your side to offer you a hand up. Though you may weep with sadness and suffer in pain, God is there to comfort you and bring healing. No matter what you are going through, God is there to help, to hold, to heal, and to love you.

June 19

The Lord is not slack concerning his promise, as some men count slackness; but is longsuffering to us-ward, not willing that any should perish, but that all should come to repentance.

–2 Peter 3:9

There is in your grace, God of second chances, insufficient evidence to prove my latest setback is a failure. Even if it is, with you, failure is never final but an opportunity to learn and grow. When I goof, as I am prone to do, help me from doubling the problem by failing to take advantage of your redemption.

June 20

Lord, sometimes I long to stand out. I notice others with shinier hair, amazing figures, and impeccable outfits, and I feel so plain. At these times, help me to remember that I should be at work cultivating the gentle and quiet spirit that is precious to you. This type of spirit may not call out, "Here I am!" but over the long run, it accomplishes much. I am doing what I can, and I leave the rest to you. I trust that you will bring all to fruition.

June 21

Behold, how good and how pleasant it is for brethren to dwell together in unity!

–Psalm 133:1

As spring turns into summer, I thank God for granting me friends with whom to share nature's bounty.

June 22

Then they cry unto the Lord in
their trouble, and he bringeth them out
of their distresses. He maketh the
storm a calm, so that the waves thereof
are still. Then are they glad
because they be quiet; so he bringeth
them unto their desired haven.

–Psalm 107:28-30

Prayer can move mountains, they say. But
I've never seen a mountain budge...except in
an earthquake or volcanic eruption. The results of persistent prayer can have the same
earthshaking, explosive results.

June 23

My Aim Is...

    to please him through communing in prayer
    to show his love and for others care
    to read his Word as my guide for life
    to cease my grumbling that causes strife
    to be open to God's leading and his will
    to take time to meditate, be quiet, and still
    to continually grow in my Christlike walk
    to be more like Jesus in my life and my talk.

June 24

Take heed to yourselves:
If thy brother trespass against thee,
rebuke him; and if he repent, forgive him.

–Luke 17:3

God, I pray for the strength and the wisdom to know what to do in this situation. I pray for enough love to forgive this person for the pain they have caused me and to forgive myself for the ill will I have harbored against this person. Help me be a truly forgiving person so that the weight of resentment may be lifted from my shoulders. Amen.

June 25

Father, please remind me throughout my day that this moment is all I have in which to live. I can't retrieve or retract anything I've done or said just ten minutes ago. Nor can I be sure of what will happen ten minutes hence. So I pray, Lord, help me leave the past and the future with you so that I can experience the peace of your love in this important bit of eternity called "now."

June 26

Lift up your heart in
sweet surrender to the
God who is waiting
to shower you with
blessings. Lift up your
soul on wings of joy to
the God who is waiting
to guide you from the
chaos of shadows out
into the light of a peace
that knows no equal.

June 27

We respond to stresses in our lives with either fear or faith. Fear is a great threat to our faith. That's why we read often in the scriptures the directive, "Fear not." The closer we draw to God, the more our fears diminish.

June 28

Waiting,
endless waiting.
Why does it seem impossible
to wait patiently
and
graciously—
> for the overdue phone call
> or the long-expected letter...
> for delayed company to arrive
> or a sick loved one to get better?
Is there a special ingredient
to fill the waiting time
and ease the heavy burdens
that weigh upon my mind?

Could waiting possibly achieve a work
which nothing else can do?
God, teach me how to
wait patiently
and put full trust
in you.

June 29

Lying lips are abomination to the Lord:
but they that deal truly are his delight.

–Proverbs 12:22

We can never be completely honest on our own. It is human nature to lie. That's why when a witness who takes the stand in a court of law is asked, "Do you solemnly swear to tell the truth, the whole truth, and nothing but the truth," the phrase is added, "so help me God."

June 30

Nothing thrills the heart and awakens the spirit like a summer thunderstorm, alive with electric energy and thick with potential danger. With each explosive boom of thunder and blinding flash of lightning, our adrenaline rises and our hair stands on end. Without a reminder of our deep connection to the natural world, we can grow dull and lifeless, stiff and anxious, lost and uncertain. Then the thunder roars and the lightning pierces the dark sky, and we remember once again that we are all a part of something far grander and more awesome than we could ever imagine.

July

July 1

> *A man's heart deviseth his way:*
> *but the Lord directeth his steps.*
>
> *—Proverbs 16:9*

A despairing heart mumbles, "God is doing nothing."
A hopeful heart inquires, "God, what are you going
to do next?" and looks forward to celebrating God's
awesome ingenuity.

July 2

God hears my cries for help, and
He answers every prayer.
I only need be patient—
He supplies the "how" and "where."

Sometimes it may be immediate
In a tangible way I'll know;
While other times I wait assured
That he is strengthening my soul.

His grace is all-sufficient
To meet my heart-cries need.
As I lean upon his promises,
Walking in faith, he'll lead.

July 3

*For I am persuaded, that neither death,
nor life, nor angels, nor principalities,
nor powers, nor things present,
nor things to come. Nor height, nor depth,
nor any other creature, shall be able
to separate us from the love of God, which
is in Christ Jesus our Lord.*

—Romans 8:38-39

Faith in God's love frees me to be the real me, for I remember that God sees me as I am and loves me with all his heart.

July 4

How blessed I am to live in the United States! Life may not always be easy, but I am grateful for the freedoms this nation gives to me. Thank you, Lord, for all the people who fought to make this country a free and beautiful land. I remember those patriots today as I listen to fireworks and enjoy my freedom. May I never take that freedom for granted.

July 5

And, behold, I am with thee,
and will keep thee in all places whither thou
goest, and will bring thee again into this
land; for I will not leave thee, until I have
done that which I have spoken to thee of.

—Genesis 28:15

Teach us to know, God, that it is exactly at the point of our deepest despair that you are closest. For at those times we can finally admit we have wandered in the dark, without a clue. Yet you have been there with us all along. Thank you for your abiding presence.

July 6

Thank heaven for summer rain!
Through the pall of the sweltering sky,
It falls like kisses to the earth,
Renewing and nourishing.
Like a child
I run—
Arms open,
Face to the clouds,
Into the downpour.
All around the people hide
Under doorways and umbrellas,
While the rain pours down on me,
Washing away my gloom.

Although our eyes should always be turned above toward God, sometimes we can do with a reminder of God's work just a little bit closer to home. The faith of others can serve as a reminder or an inspiration to strengthen our own faith. Just as we should provide encouragement to others, we can draw on others to help steady ourselves.

July 8

> *And I heard a great voice out of heaven saying, Behold, the tabernacle of God is with men, and he will dwell with them, and they shall be his people, and God himself shall be with them, and be their God.*
>
> *—Revelation 21:3*

We don't really know why we have to get sick, Lord. We only know your promise: No matter where we are or what we are called to endure, there you are in the midst of it with us, never leaving our side. Not for a split second. Thank you, Lord of all.

Finally, my brethren, be strong in the Lord, and in the power of his might.

—Ephesians 6:10

God is bigger than any problem you have. Whoever is opposing you is a weakling compared to God. Why not tap into God's supply of strength? Why focus on your problem when God is so much more interesting?

July 10

Hope opens our hearts
And lessens our woes.
It fights against strife
And vanquishes foes.
It can be as small as a smile
Or as long as the day.
It's a gift that grows larger
When you give it away.

July 11

If I can throw a single ray of light across the darkened pathway of another; if I can aid some soul to clearer sight of life and duty, and thus bless my brother; if I can wipe from any human cheek a tear, I shall not have lived my life in vain while here.

July 12

I am still moving, God, through storms. By your grace—over rough country, you have carried me; amidst pounding waves, you have held me; beyond the horizon of my longings you have shown me your purposes. Even in this small room, sitting still, I am moving, God. Closer.

July 13

Therefore, my beloved brethren, be ye stead-fast, unmovable, always abounding in the work of the Lord, forasmuch as ye know that your labour is not in vain in the Lord.

—1 Corinthians 15:58

We can take a lesson from the precious water lily. For no matter what outside force or pressure is put upon the lily, it always rises back to the water's surface again to feel the nurturing sunlight upon its leaves and petals. We must be like the lily, steadfast and true in the face of every difficulty, that we too may rise above our problems and feel God's light upon our faces again.

July 14

*And thou shalt love the Lord thy God
with all thine heart, and with all thy soul,
and with all thy might.*

—Deuteronomy 6:5

God wants us to love him, not because he is greedy for love, but because when we are devoted to loving him, we get in touch with his powerful, everlasting love for us. When we do, we cannot contain it, and it overflows to others.

July 15

> *Thou shalt not go up and down as a talebearer among thy people: neither shalt thou stand against the blood of thy neighbour; I am the Lord. Thou shalt not hate thy brother in thine heart: thou shalt in any wise rebuke thy neighbour, and not suffer sin upon him. Thou shalt not avenge, nor bear any grudge against the children of thy people, but thou shalt love thy neighbour as thyself: I am the Lord.*
>
> *—Leviticus 19:16-18*

Fear and lack of understanding can prevent us from loving our neighbor. If we pray for his assistance, God will help us reach out to our neighbor with his love.

July 16

Most of us realize that we are naturally self-centered, and we often respond to those around us in ways that make us appear proud, haughty, or arrogant. But if we look at Jesus' life, we see an excellent example of humility—an example that we should strive to follow. He taught that pride was destructive, but humility was powerful. Rather than touting his own greatness, Jesus was willing to kneel down and wash the feet of others, to show that we should all be servants to each other—and to God.

For years
I was afraid
To approach you—
afraid you'd disapprove of me
or declare me "unacceptable."

When I finally sought you,
I discovered you were tender,
compassionate, loving.
Now instead of fear,
during my life's purest moments,
I feel secure,
embraced,
totally accepted—
and completely loved by you.

July 18

> *Fear thou not; for I am with thee:*
> *be not dismayed; for I am thy God: I will*
> *strengthen thee; yea, I will help thee;*
> *yea, I will uphold thee with the right hand*
> *of my righteousness.*
>
> —Isaiah 41:10

No matter what my ears may hear
Or what my eyes may see,
There's nothing for me to fear, Lord;
You're always here with me.

July 19

*If we confess our sins, he is faithful
and just to forgive us our sins, and to cleanse
us from all unrighteousness.*

–1 John 1:9

Forgive us, Lord, our sins, for failing to live up to
your standards of goodness and justice. We confess
our shortcomings. Make us willing to change and
help us become persons of godly character. Amen.

July 20

The Lord is my rock, and my fortress, and my deliverer; my God, my strength, in whom I will trust; my buckler, and the horn of my salvation, and my high tower.

—Psalm 18:2

God, I know that you close some doors in my life in order to open new ones. I know that things change and come to an end in order to leave room for new beginnings. Help me have the boldness and enthusiasm to let go of the old and accept the new. Amen.

We all have numerous resources from which to share. Having a "generous spirit" does not mean simply giving money. Time is another precious commodity, and generous volunteers enable many organizations to function well: hospitals, schools, missions, animal shelters, community centers, nursing homes, child-care centers, churches—and the list goes on. Look around. What do you have to share? A "spirit of generosity" means open-handedly giving time, energy, and creativity, as well as monetary resources. Great is the reward of the person who generously gives whatever he or she has to help others.

July 22

God, I know you're not in a hurry—
Your plans for me are on time.
You need no schedule or reminders
For I'm always on your mind.

I know you have drawn the mosaic
And you're fitting each tile in place.
As I continue to follow your plan,
Help me not to hurry or race.

Waiting is so often difficult,
And patience I don't easily learn.
But to have my life more Christ-like
Is for what I seek and yearn.

So as my life's pattern continues
And the next part begins to unfold,
It's you I'm trusting and praising,
It's your hand I cling to and hold.

> *Heaviness in the heart of man maketh it stoop: but a good word maketh it glad.*
>
> *—Proverbs 12:25*

Lord, the clamor of my life is unbearable. People pressing in on all sides. Decisions crying out to be made. Problems needing to be solved. I don't want to get out of bed in the morning. I want to hide, to escape. Please help me!

July 24

An honest man is not a man who never lies. There is no such man. When an honest man is caught in a lie or discovers he has lied, he is quick to admit it. He then speaks the truth. He's not afraid to say, "Please forgive me for not being honest." He does not defend a lie. Unlike a dishonest man, he does not make plans to lie or use lies to cover other falsehoods. He regularly scrutinizes his life to see if he has lied or is living a lie in any area. Honesty with God, his fellow man, and himself is the honest man's goal and his heart's desire.

July 25

Dear Lord, my financial demands exceed the resources I have. The pressure I feel to do something, even if it's unwise, is building, and I fear I will cave in and make a decision I will regret. Help me trust you. Preserve my integrity and show me your way of dealing with this situation.

July 26

> *O Lord, how manifold are thy works!*
> *In wisdom hast thou made them all:*
> *the earth is full of thy riches.*
>
> *—Psalm 104:24*

The creative power within is your power to overcome any obstacle and break through any binding walls that keep you from your dreams. This power was given to you by the greatest of all creators, the one who created you, God. Just look around at the amazing beauty and diversity of the world you live in, and you will never again doubt that God supports your creative endeavors.

July 27

Like a speed bump in a parking lot, a decision lies in our path, placed there by God to remind us hope is a choice. Choosing to live as people of hope is not to diminish or belittle pain and suffering or lie about evil's reality. Rather it is to cling to God's promise that he will make all things new.

July 28

Peace is about releasing.
It's about opening my hand
and letting go of my plan,
my agenda,
my demands
on God and other people
and even on myself.
It's about realizing
that every person
is as important as I am
in God's eyes.
It's remembering
I don't know everything
and I don't have solutions
to every problem.
It's about calling on
the one who does.

July 29

> *Praise ye the Lord. Praise the Lord,*
> *O my soul. While I live will I*
> *praise the Lord: I will sing praises unto*
> *my God while I have any being.*
>
> *—Psalm 146:1-2*

Thank you, Lord, for reaching out and drawing me under your wings. Even though I am just one of billions of people who need you, your love is so great that you know my troubles, are concerned for my welfare, and are working to renew my dreams. I am so blessed to have you to turn to when I am faced with a calamity, and I am so very grateful that I have you to lean on. I praise you with all my heart. Amen.

July 30

To serve means to assist or be of use. Serving is one of the reasons we are on this earth and the reason Jesus himself said he came to the earth. When we serve, we reach out to meet the needs of others; service is an outward sign that we belong to God and desire to do his will. True service is not about grudgingly doing for others because of obligation, but an act that flows willingly, as a channel for God's love. True servants give not just with their hands, but with their hearts.

Two are better than one; because they have a good reward for their labour. For if they fall, the one will lift up his fellow: but woe to him that is alone when he falleth; for he hath not another to help him up.

—Ecclesiastes 4:9-10

The words "alone," "lonely," and "abandoned" all contain the word "one." When we believe we stand by ourselves to face life's difficulties—just one person against the world—we will often feel alone, lonely, and abandoned. But in the words "community," "fellowship," and "family," there is no longer the possibility that one might be left to stand alone.

August

August 1

Dear God, shine through me and help me lighten another's darkness by showing the same friendship that you extended. Show me a person that is in desperate need of a friend today. Help me to be sensitive, caring, and willing to go out of my way to meet this person's need right now, whether it be emotional, physical, or spiritual. Thank you that when I need a friend, you are the friend that sticketh closer than a brother. In Jesus' name, Amen.

August 2

I love the Lord, because he hath heard my voice and my supplications. Because he hath inclined his ear unto me, therefore will I call upon him as long as I live.

—Psalm 116:1-2

In the depth of my pain, I cry out to God. In grief and sorrow, in loss and anguish, I cry out to God. When I am overwhelmed and cannot bear another moment, I cry out to God. And he hears my cry. He listens and cares and answers, as he always has throughout all time.

August 3

Dear God, I know that I have wronged others over the course of the years. I pray that those moments are long forgotten, and if they are not, I pray that I might somehow make them right. I truly forgive anyone who has wronged me, letting go of any grudges or hurtful feelings. And I pray that as I forgive, so may I be forgiven. Amen.

August 4

God, I couldn't help noticing all the loveliness you placed in the world today! This morning I witnessed a sunrise that made my heart beat faster. Then, later, I watched a father gently help his child across a busy parking lot; his tenderness was much like yours. While inside a department store, I spied an elderly couple sitting on a bench. I could hear the man cracking jokes; their laughter lifted my spirits. Then early this evening, I walked by a woman tending her flower bed; she took great pleasure in her work, and her garden was breathtaking. Later, I talked with a friend who is helping some needy families; her genuine compassion inspired me. Thank you, Lord, for everything that is beautiful and good in the world.

August 5

Verily, verily, I say unto you, The servant is not greater than his lord; neither he that is sent greater than he that sent him.

—John 13:16

Heavenly Father, it is good to remember that everything that lives and breathes is sacred to you. We must never feel superior to any other human being—for we are all precious in your eyes. You have given us life, and we must make the choices that lead to kindness and peace. You created us, but how we live together is up to us. Thank you.

August 6

> *Create in me a clean heart, O God; and renew a right spirit within me.*
>
> *–Psalm 51:10*

Father God, we know that to receive the blessing of healing, the heart must be open. But when we are mad, we close off the heart as if it were a prison. Remind us that a heart that is shut cannot receive understanding, acceptance, and renewal. Even though we feel angry, we must keep the heart's door slightly ajar so your grace can enter and fill our darkness with the light of hope.

August 7

> *We are troubled on every side, yet not*
> *distressed; we are perplexed, but*
> *not in despair; Persecuted, but not forsaken;*
> *cast down, but not destroyed.*
>
> *–2 Corinthians 4:8-9*

Father, make me resilient like the sandy beach upon which the waves crash. Make me strong like the mighty willow tree that bends but does not break in the high winds. Give me the patience and wisdom to know that my suffering will one day turn to a greater understanding of your ways, your works, and your wonders.

August 8

The Lord is my shepherd; I shall not want.

–Psalm 23:1

Sometimes I feel abandoned, Lord. I feel empty inside, and it's hard to connect with myself, with others, and with the world. I almost lose faith at these times, Lord. Please stay with me and help me remember your love, your light, and your peace.

August 9

Stop moaning and asking, "Why, God, why?"
There is always a meaningful reason.
Stop whining and pleading, "When, God, when?"
For good things will arrive in due season.
We are promised that God's never early,
But neither is God ever late.
All the blessings we wish will come to us
When we learn to have faith while we wait.
When I am lost and discouraged,
And there seems to be no hope in sight,
I turn my cares over to the God of my heart,
And his love lets my spirit take flight.

August 10

We all prefer to deal with honest people—people we can trust—people who will not lie or try to deceive us. A noble goal for one's life is to pursue honesty—honesty with others, with ourselves, and with God. Yet it is not natural to tell the truth. Honesty can seem to leave us open to attack—to tear down the walls of protection we would rather erect in our lives. Scripture tells us, "The truth shall make you free." Although it might be hard to be honest, if we do it with loving intentions, the burden that dishonesty brings will be lifted.

August 11

Life's not fair, and I stomp my foot in frustration. The powerful get more so as the rest of us shrink, dreams for peace are shattered as bullies get the upper hand, and despair is a tempting pit to fall into. Help me hold on, for you are a God of justice and dreams, of turning life upside down. Let me help; thanks for listening in the meantime.

August 12

> *But let him ask in faith, nothing wavering. For he that wavereth is like a wave of the sea driven with the wind and tossed.*
>
> *–James 1:6*

Sometimes my doubts are so strong and so bothersome. Give me courage to express my doubts to you, O God, knowing that they are necessary moments through which I can pass on my way to true contentment in you.

August 13

> *Let your light so shine before men,*
> *that they may see your good works,*
> *and glorify your Father which is in heaven.*
>
> *–Matthew 5:16*

In this day of bigger is best, Lord, we wonder what difference our little lights can make. Remind us of the laser, so tiny, yet when focused, has infinite power. This little light of mine, O Lord, give it such focus.

August 14

Human beings are the only creatures that strive to be something they are not. Perhaps we should take a lesson from the birds of the sky, who never ache to be anything other than creatures able to fly at will upon a lifting breeze. Or we should learn from the fish of the sea, who don't doubt their own ability to glide through blue waters dappled with sunlight. Or maybe we should spend some time watching wild horses thunder over the open plains, and we would see that not once do they stop to wish they were anything more than what God made them: glorious, beautiful, and free.

August 15

And be not conformed to this world: but be ye transformed by the renewing of your mind, that ye may prove what is that good, and acceptable, and perfect, will of God.

–Romans 12:2

I get discouraged, O God, my comforter and guide, and feel overwhelmed, which makes me even more discouraged. Lead me beyond negative thoughts and useless circles of worry to a renewed frame of mind. Work your miracle of transformation in me.

August 16

Lord, I am weary and cannot find my way. The nights seem endless and thick with a fog that engulfs my spirit, but I have faith in you, my Lord and my light. Faith that you will help me take another step when I feel I can no longer walk on my own. Faith that you will be the beacon of hope that guides my way through the darkness. Faith that this, too, shall pass and that I will know joy again. Amen.

August 17

Just when I settle in with one reality, something new disrupts. Overnight change, God of all the time in the world, is comforting and grief-making, for it's a reminder that nothing stays the same. Not tough times, not good ones either. Despite today's annoyance, I'm grateful for change, assured it will take me to new moments you have in mind.

August 18

Sticks and stones of prejudice feel like they're breaking bones. Yet God calls us by name, numbers the hairs on our heads, guards our comings in and goings out, lifts us to high places and sets angels over us. How can we doubt our value with such overwhelming evidence to the contrary!

August 19

Be of good courage, and he shall strengthen your heart, all ye that hope in the Lord.

–Psalm 31:24

Help me understand, Lord, that the courage I am praying for is not dry-eyed stoicism and perky denial. Courage is not hiding my feelings, even from you, and putting on a brave false face. Rather it is facing facts, weighing options, and moving ahead. No need to waste precious time pretending.

August 20

A merry heart doeth good like a medicine:
but a broken spirit drieth the bones.

–Proverbs 17:22

As we face worrisome days, restore our funny bones, Lord. Humor helps rebuild and heal, sparking hope and igniting energy with which to combat stress, ease grief, and provide direction.

August 21

Lord, you've given me a great team of helpers,
And I'm exceedingly thankful.
Where would I be without them?
They seem to know my needs before I do,
And they jump to meet them.
I know you've given them those gifts of caring,
Of encouragement, of hospitality and healing,
But they're using those gifts as you intended,
To show your love to others—I mean me.
I am thankful to you and to them.
There's not much I can do to pay them back, Lord.
They'd probably refuse a reward anyway.
So I ask you to shower them with blessings,
Just as they have brought blessing to me.
Give them joy and peace in rich supply,
And let your love continue to flow
To them, within them, and through them.
Amen.

August 22

Your Word really does cut to the heart of the matter
when it comes to what life is about, Lord. It doesn't
let me hide behind excuses, pretenses, or lies. It
gives me the straight scoop without any meaning-
less frills. That kind of honesty is hard to find in
this world—especially accompanied by the absolute
love that fuels it. As you lay open my heart with
your truth, help me not to run and hide; help me to
trust your love enough to allow you to complete the
"surgery" that will bring the health and well-being
my soul longs for.

August 23

Thou shalt have no other gods before me.

–Exodus 20:3

Lord, please keep me from falling into the trap of placing any other human on a pedestal. Even the most spiritual-seeming religious leaders are riddled with imperfection; they struggle with sin, just as I do. You alone are perfect and pure, and you alone are worthy of my adoration. I promise I will not follow anyone else, no matter how spiritually enlightened they may seem. There is no one like you, and you are the only one who will ever have my full devotion.

August 24

In my attempts to "get it right" as I order my life and the lives of those in my family, remind me, O Creator God, to look around and see how you have brought order to our world. Such balance, such harmony, such stability. May I find the faith to trust you like a bird trusts the winds that allow it to soar.

August 25

Regardless of what the future holds, I'm savoring all sorts of wondrous things I've been too busy to notice before. A thousand daily marvels bring a smile to my face. Through your grace, Lord, rather than thinking how sad it is that I missed them before, I'm delighted to be seeing, doing them now. These small wonders energize me, and for that I'm thankful. It's never too late to be a joyful explorer.

August 26

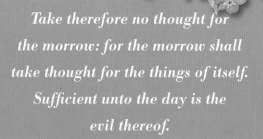

Take therefore no thought for the morrow: for the morrow shall take thought for the things of itself. Sufficient unto the day is the evil thereof.

—Matthew 6:34

Lord, sometimes I worry about my loved ones. Though I often complain of the monotony of my day-to-day life, I know my days are full of moments to be treasured. When I hear shocking, horrific stories on the news, I often wonder how I would handle such events if they were to befall me or a loved one. Father, I cling to your promise that you give each of us a future filled with hope. I am grateful that you hear me when I come to you in prayer. Please stay close to me and my loved ones. Grant us the strength to prevail in all circumstances.

August 27

O Lord, I savor this triumph: I met my goal! Day by day, I reached into my heart and found energy to keep on. Day by day, I reached out and found your hand leading, your inspiration guiding. Stand with me to accept applause for our joint success.

August 28

Blessed be the God and Father of our Lord Jesus Christ, who hath blessed us with all spiritual blessings in heavenly places in Christ.

–Ephesians 1:3

Lord, no matter what we bring of ourselves to give you, even if we include all our hopes and dreams, it's never enough to give in return for all you've given to us. And so we give you our praise. We sing to you and come before you with our meager offerings, praying all the while that you will make something marvelous of them.

August 29

Prioritizing spiritual realities over temporal ones is not always easy. The physical realities are tangible. I can hold a stack of bills in my hand and know that if I don't pay them, problems will arise. But those spiritual realities... well, the benefits (and consequences) are not always so easy to recognize or see in the moment. This is a faith issue, pure and simple. First, I need to stay calm about issues of pro-vision. Second, I need to keep drawing near to you. Third, I need to reach out to others with your love. And after all of these things are done, I need to trust you with the results.

August 30

Lord, what compassion you showered on your people when you grouped us into families! Thank you,
Lord, for the homes we are privileged to
enjoy. We are thankful for these
sanctuaries for our children
and grandchildren. May
our homes and our families
honor you, Lord, in all we
say and do within them.
Dwell with us, Lord. You
are always welcome.

August 31

> *But thanks be to God,*
> *which giveth us the victory through*
> *our Lord Jesus Christ.*
>
> *—1 Corinthians 15:57*

Lord, I just want to tell you how much I love you, how grateful I am that you have taken me into your care. Ever since I've entrusted myself to you, you've kept me from becoming entangled in the kinds of things that would bring me to ruin. You fill my heart and mind with peace as I stay close to you. It's a miracle of your grace that I am standing tall today, lifting my praise to you from a heart full of love.

September

September 1

Father,

It's easy to say, "Let me know if there's anything I can do." But how much better to peer closer, assess the situation to find what needs doing...then simply do it. Help me look into a friend's needs instead of waiting to be asked. Help me replace the words I utter so glibly with actions that might matter even more.

Amen.

September 2

O God, you have called each of us to special tasks, purposes, and vocations, equipping us with the skills and energy to perform them. For some, our vocations send us into the labor force; for some, it is soon bringing retirement. For some, it is in full-time homemaking. For some, our vocations are in artistic skills; for some, in volunteering, helping, neighboring. Always, there is that first call from you, God of vision, working through our work to help, heal, change a needful world.

September 3

And even to your old age I am he; and even to hoar hairs will I carry you: I have made, and I will bear; even I will carry, and will deliver you.

—Isaiah 46:4

Lord, I wish to live a long life, but I fear growing old. I want to accomplish great things, but I fear risking what I already have. I desire to love with all my heart, but the prospect of self-revelation makes me shrink back. Perhaps for just this day, you would help me reach out? Let me bypass these dreads and see instead your hand reaching back to mine—right now—just as it always has.

September 4

We're stained, like a paint rag, by troubles we caused ourselves, Lord. Red, the color of lost temper and rudeness. Green, envy of others who have it easier and more of it. Blue, the shade of despair over something we could change. Yellow, of cowardly running. Rearrange our unsightly smudges into glorious rainbows through your gift of forgiveness.

September 5

What, God of peace, are we to do with our anger? In the wake of trouble, it fills us to overflowing. Sometimes our anger is the only prayer we can bring you. We are relieved and grateful to know that you are sturdy enough to bear all we feel and say. Where do we go from here? Is there life after fury? What will we be without our anger when it's all that has fueled us? When we are still, we hear your answer: "Emptied." But then we would be nothing. Remind us that, in your redeeming hands, nothing can become of great use, as a gourd hollowed out becomes a cup or a bowl only when emptied. When the time comes for us to empty ourselves of this abundance of anger, make us into something useful. It would be a double tragedy to waste anger's re-creative energy.

September 6

Bless my family, O God, for it is unique . . . some say too much so. I am grateful you know we are joined by love—for each other and for and from you. We are grateful you use more than one pattern to create a good family. This pioneering family has you at its heart.

September 7

Lord, it's hard to hit a target with closed eyes, yet I approach you blindly. Help me see that faith is not a quantity that can be measured like gas in a tank but a gift, a quality, that says, "I believe God is for me, not against me."

September 8

I know that my character is what I am in the dark, when no one is watching, and no one can see. For this reason, bless me in my solitude. Because temptation is the greatest here, and the possibility of a setback looms large.

September 9

The surge of adrenaline as we look over our shoulders to see who's gaining on us is as natural as breathing, Lord, and we pick up the pace to keep ahead. If behind, we dig in to overtake whoever is ahead of us. Competition is exhilarating, and we welcome its challenges. Yet, competition out of control creates bare-knuckle conflict within us, and we are shocked at the lengths to which we will go to win. Help us weigh the risks and benefits of getting a corner office, promotion, and raise. Keep us achieving, Lord, for being the best, brightest, and boldest is a worthy goal. Help us win fair and square and not cheat ourselves. Help us remember that we can best gain the competitive edge by focusing on your guidance. And how, really, can we see where you are leading if we are walking backward on the lookout for whoever might be overtaking us! That is losing, no matter what we win.

September 10

The fear of man bringeth a snare: but whoso putteth his trust in the Lord shall be safe.

–Proverbs 29:25

Lord, fear has reared its ugly head again and is trying to take me far away from you. Hold me close, Lord. Even though I have momentarily lost my footing in this world, please do not let fear steal the peace I find in you. Give me the strength to turn away from fear and stand tall in the knowledge that I am never alone.

September 11

This is a sad and solemn day, yet there is still time to be thankful. Thank you, Lord, for all the emergency workers who help people every day. They bring light to the darkness and help to those who need it most. Thank you for their selflessness and willingness to give everything they have to save another. Just as Jesus sacrificed his life to save us, we are blessed by the sacrifices of those who save our lives.

September 12

> *And he said unto them, Take heed,*
> *and beware of covetousness: for a man's life*
> *consisteth not in the abundance of the*
> *things which he possesseth.*
>
> –Luke 12:15

Father, you've shown me that coveting isn't always as straightforward as wishing I had someone else's house or car. The covetous corruption that creeps in can wear any number of disguises, such as begrudging the fact that someone has been blessed in some way that I haven't. It can be despising someone else's success or hoping for their failure so I won't feel left behind. The list goes on, but the essence is my discontent with my own lot in life as I compare myself with someone else. Set me free today to enjoy the blessings you've provided without spoiling them by pointless comparisons.

September 13

Lord, how much time do we spend looking into a mirror, and how often do we see you there? We were made in your image, but rather than focusing on that, we often focus on all the things we'd like to change. When others look at us, do they see our meager attempts to make our lips fuller and our eyelashes longer, or do they see the light of your love shining through our eyes? Teach us to focus less on our own appearance and concentrate more on presenting your face to those around us. It is you the world needs, not us.

September 14

God, you are so great. It is always the right time to worship you, but morning is best. Praise for the dawning light that streams in through this window. Praise for the sound of the birds as they flit through in the air. Praise for the little spider crawling along on the ceiling. Praise for the smell of coffee and the warmth of a cup in my hands. Praise for the flowering plants—and even those weeds growing by the house. Praise for the neighbors walking along the sidewalk and the clouds moving by, too. Most of all, praise for the breath that keeps flowing in and out of my lungs. Yes, this is the greatest item of praise: that you alone are my life—all life itself. Without you, all is dust. Praise . . . for you.

September 15

Father, I appreciate this encouraging reminder for me to keep chugging along the "high road." When I'm doing the right thing, it can feel like I'm going backward sometimes—especially when I see others taking not-so-ethical shortcuts and "getting ahead." I confess that when I get tired and frustrated, those shortcuts can look mighty tempting. But taking them would sabotage the good things that are ahead—the good harvest you have in mind for me to enjoy. It's not worth a temporary lapse of integrity for a bit of ill-gained ease to forfeit the fruits of good labor—labor I hope will always honor you.

September 16

I am grateful that you don't require spiritual gymnastics from me when I sin, Lord. You just call me to come to you with a humble and repentant heart. In my pride I sometimes want to do something that will impress you—something that will "make up for it" somehow. But you just shake your head and keep calling me to humble myself and bring my sincere sorrow to you. That often doesn't seem like enough to me. But I guess that's the point: I can never earn your grace; it is a gift. Christ died on the cross for us because it is beyond our powers to make up for all the sins we have committed. I bring my contrite heart before you now, Lord. Thank you for receiving it as an acceptable sacrifice.

September 17

Those people who are unlikable to me, Lord, are not worthless, though I'm tempted to believe my self-centered thoughts about them. Rather, Lord, these people are precious works of beauty, created by you. And if I bother to look beyond my first impressions, I will be delighted by what I see of you in them.

September 18

Today I will think about the miracles in my life. I am thankful that God gives me these special gifts. Miracles remind me that God is always in my life. Thank you, Lord, for showing me your power and surprising me with these moments of grace. Help me see your hand at work and trust that your way is the best.

September 19

Good morning, Lord. I have another busy day ahead of me. This may be the only minute I have to talk to you. Please tap me on the shoulder now and then—no matter how busy I am—and remind me that the world does not revolve around me.

September 20

What a day. When all else fails, rearrange the furniture. Lend a shoulder, God of change, as I scoot the couch to a new spot. Like wanderers to your promised land, I need a fresh perspective. My life has turned top-sy-turvy, and I need a new place to sit . . . first with you, then the rest of my world of family, friends, job. I need to be prepared for whatever happens next, and nothing says it like a redone room. I smile as I take my new seat; this is a better view.

September 21

Dear God,
Help my unbelief.
When I'm in pain, I forget that you care about me.
I forget that you have helped me through my trials.
I forget that you hold me in your arms to keep me safe.
I forget that you are feeling my pain with me.
I forget that you love me,
I forget that I am important to you.
Show me your presence—let me feel your enveloping
love. Heal my hurting soul.
Thank you for staying with me even in my unbelief.
Amen.

September 22

Lord, I see you in the beauty of the autumn. Thank you for the brilliant colors of the trees. Thank you for the crisp, cool air that refreshes me. I am blessed to see autumn's beauty everywhere I go. Thank you for showing me that a time of change can be one of the most gorgeous seasons on Earth.

September 23

Acquaint now thyself with him, and be at peace: thereby good shall come unto thee.

–Job 22:21

Today I feel alone, yet I am not lonely. There is peace in solitude and rejuvenation in the quiet of being alone. Lead my thoughts to restful healing, Lord. Help me use this time alone to find myself and reach deep inside my heart and mind to find peace. I rejoice in being away from the noise and clatter of everyday life and praise God for letting me have this time for myself.

September 24

Security, loving God, is going to sleep in the assurance that you know our hearts before we speak and are waiting, as soon as you hear from us, to transform our concerns into hope and action, our loneliness into companionship, and our despair into dance.

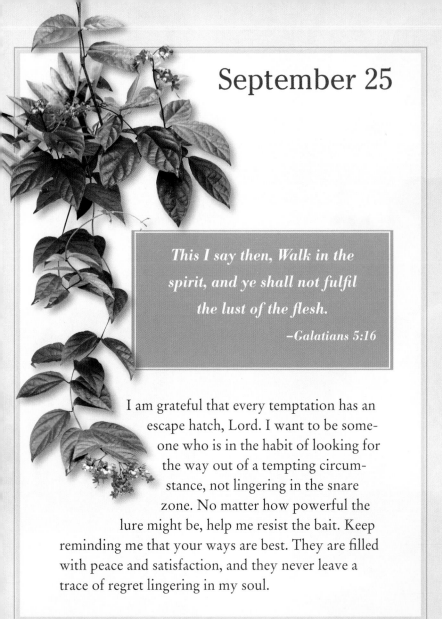

September 25

This I say then, Walk in the spirit, and ye shall not fulfil the lust of the flesh.

—Galatians 5:16

I am grateful that every temptation has an escape hatch, Lord. I want to be someone who is in the habit of looking for the way out of a tempting circumstance, not lingering in the snare zone. No matter how powerful the lure might be, help me resist the bait. Keep reminding me that your ways are best. They are filled with peace and satisfaction, and they never leave a trace of regret lingering in my soul.

September 26

Okay, Lord, I know "it's only stuff," but much of it is useful, and I want to take good care of it. Help me see the line between wanting to be a good steward and caring too much about material things. That line is often blurry from my earthly perspective. Help me be a responsible caretaker without putting too much value on mere "stuff."

September 27

In this time of change, help me to be patient, God.
Let me not run ahead of you and your plans.
Give me courage to do only what is before me and to keep
my focus on my responsibilities.
I am tempted to daydream about the future; however, the
future is in your hands.
Thus, may I be close to you in all my thoughts, accomplish
the task before me today, and do it with all my heart.

September 28

> *As far as the east is from the west, so far hath he removed our transgressions from us.*
>
> *–Psalm 103:12*

Lord, we stand in awe of your great sacrifice for us. Your journey to the cross is the reason we are free from the destruction of sin. It's why we can be forgiven and be united with you throughout eternity. No sacrifice is too great in response to your love for us. Keep us ever mindful, Lord. Keep us ever grateful.

September 29

Will there always be poor people among us? Yes. God's Word says as much, but it's not in the context of hopelessness. It's in the context of a command for us to be generous. And it's a very beautiful picture, really, of the heart of God toward all humanity. Our tangible gifts to help the poor mirror God's spiritual gifts that keep flowing toward us to meet our needs. As our hands extend food, clothing, and shelter to those who lack it, God's hands extend grace, mercy, and forgiveness to give us all that our needy souls lack.

September 30

In all things, give thanks. In the good days of laughter and joy, give thanks.
In the bad days of struggle and strife, give thanks.
In the brightest moments and the darkest hours, give thanks.
In the flow of blessings and the apparent lack of goodness, give thanks.
In the face of fortune and misfortune, give thanks.
In the presence of pleasure and pain, give thanks.
In all things, give thanks.
For lessons and blessings are found not just in the light, but in the darkness.

October

October 1

When I'm bored, remind me:
This is the excitement of life—
darkness alternating with light,
down dancing with up,
and inactivity being absolutely essential
—as prelude—
to the most fulfilling experiences of all.

October 2

Your Word says—and I've heard it elsewhere—that a flock of sheep knows its own shepherd's voice and won't respond to the voice of a different shepherd. It's true of my relationship with you, too, Lord: I know your voice. I know when you're speaking to my heart, and I know when I'm being coaxed by "other voices"—wrong desires, worldly values, anxiety, pride, and the like. Thanks for helping me see the difference. Coax me to follow the sound of your voice today and always.

October 3

Stumbling happens. Don't I know it! I can get bummed out just by reviewing my mistakes and mess-ups from yesterday. But thankfully, I don't need to! God has hold of my hand. My worst blunders—even if they've been truly harmful to myself or others—are not the end of the world. God will bring a new day, a fresh start, a redeemed relationship, a restored soul.

October 4

In the multitude of words there wanteth not sin: but he that refraineth his lips is wise.

—Proverbs 10:19

Lord, I knew the minute the words were out of my mouth that they would have been better left unsaid. Why do I continue to fall into the trap of needing to say what I think at the expense of someone else? Not only did I hurt someone's feelings, but I also looked like a fool in the process! Help me to repair the damage and learn from this experience. Give me another chance to behave nobly by saying nothing.

October 5

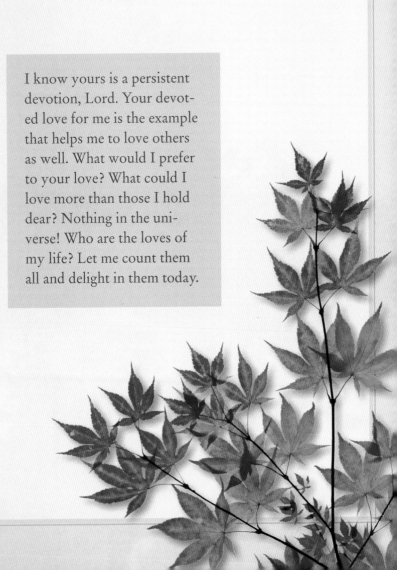

I know yours is a persistent devotion, Lord. Your devoted love for me is the example that helps me to love others as well. What would I prefer to your love? What could I love more than those I hold dear? Nothing in the universe! Who are the loves of my life? Let me count them all and delight in them today.

October 6

Almighty God, of all the things you've created, friendship must be among your favorites. What a joy it is for me to be with my good friends, Lord. What encouragement and affirmation I get from them—and what correction if it's needed!

I cried when one of my dearest friends told me they were moving two states away, but you, O Lord, have kept us close in heart. That's the beauty of true friendship. It isn't just for here and now. It's forever.

October 7

Lord, in your infinite wisdom you knew we would need instruction for life, and so you placed in your Word the guidelines for living a productive life that brings you glory. Your Word nurtures us body and soul and keeps our minds focused on the beautiful, positive aspects of life. Thank you, Lord, for not leaving us here without a guidebook. We'd be lost without your Word.

October 8

*Be patient therefore, brethren,
unto the coming of the Lord. Behold,
the husbandman waiteth for
the precious fruit of the earth, and
hath long patience for it, until he
receive the early and latter rain.*

—James 5:7

Waiting? Waiting is not my forte, Father. As someone who has a hard time waiting for the microwave to heat my lunch, waiting for your answers to prayer is sometimes excruciating. But I've come to see that these waiting periods are usually good for me. I grow in discipline, and I discover the peace of your presence.

October 9

Lord, the last thing I want to say to the person who tailgates me in traffic is "Bless you." And I certainly don't want to pray for him or her to have a good day. Oh, but how graciously you've blessed my life, even though I've acted like a jerk on countless occasions. So please help me to peel my focus off of how I'm being treated and redirect it toward how I've been treated by you. Then I'll be able to draw from your great reservoir of mercy and pay it forward in the form of a blessing instead of a curse.

October 10

Today I'll simply trust you, Father. I'll remember that you're not looking for résumés full of impressive credentials; rather, you seek hearts that trust in you. You want to enjoy a vibrant, meaningful relationship with me—a relationship in which I trust you fully. That's the starting point of a life lived for you.

October 11

Victories—both big and small—are sweet when they come from you, God. Promotions, honors, breakthroughs, discoveries, answered prayers... it's fun to savor them and know that your gracious hand has provided them. Help me remember to thank you when I taste victory today and to give you praise in all circumstances. My greatest reward in this life is your abiding presence with me.

October 12

Jesus said unto him, If thou canst believe, all things are possible to him that believeth.

—Mark 9:23

Trying to tackle life without God is like making your way alone through a dense jungle filled with all sorts of perils. It is rough going—discouraging, disheartening, and often disastrous. On the other hand, the life of faith is one of being led on a well-kept path. Even though trouble may come along, it cannot overwhelm us because the Lord strengthens and guards our souls when we call on him for help.

October 13

Take heed, brethren, lest there be in any of you an evil heart of unbelief, in departing from the living God. But exhort one another daily, while it is called To day; lest any of you be hardened through the deceitfulness of sin. For we are made partakers of Christ, if we hold the beginning of our confidence steadfast unto the end.

–Hebrews 3:12-14

I remember hearing someone say once, "If God seems far away, guess who moved?" It's true, Lord: Sometimes I drift far away from you. I neglect reading your Word, I let my prayer life go by the wayside, and I get all tangled up in my attempts to handle everything on my own. I usually come to a sudden realization of how much I need you, and I am grateful for the epiphany! Even though I'm the one who's moved so far away, you don't hold it against me; you simply call me back.

October 14

Lord, so often the difference between a productive workday and a fruitless one lies in our attitude. When we truly work as if working for you, it makes such a wonderful difference! Forgive us, Lord, for those times when we dig into our tasks without bringing you into the situation as well. Whether it's peeling potatoes, pulling weeds, or writing a screenplay, we want to tune into your power to perfect our work on this earth.

October 15

Forgiveness is a supernatural response to being wronged. Would we know what forgiveness is if God had not shown us by first forgiving us? It seems highly unlikely. That's why real forgiveness—the kind that God extends to us—can only come through God's grace. In our own strength, we may try to forgive someone over and over again, only to call to mind the offense later (for perhaps the hundredth time). But when we ask God to open our hearts, he fills them with his love and makes us capable of full forgiveness.

October 16

Love not the world, neither the things that are in the world. If any man love the world, the love of the Father is not in him. For all that is in the world, the lust of the flesh, and the lust of the eyes, and the pride of life, is not of the Father, but is of the world. And the world passeth away, and the lust thereof: but he that doeth the will of God abideth for ever.

–1 John 2:15-17

Father God, you are the giver of all gifts. All of our resources and all we have came from you, and they are only ours for a little while. Protect us from any addiction to material things, Lord. Gently remind us when we have enough—enough to eat, enough to wear, enough to enjoy. Most of all, keep us mindful of the fact that because we have you, we have everything we need.

October 17

Someone may ask, "What's the difference between humility and humiliation?" A simple way to look at it is that humility is voluntary and peaceful, while humiliation is compulsory and painful. Practically speaking, it's better for me to think rightly about myself in relation to God and others (i.e., to walk in humility) than to think I'm "all that" and experience the humiliation of an extreme reality check. As I walk in true humility, there's the added bonus that God will send honor my way—and the honor he will set up for me will be sweeter than any I could try to grab for myself.

October 18

Finally, brethren, whatsoever things are true, whatsoever things are honest, whatsoever things are just, whatsoever things are pure, whatsoever things are lovely, whatsoever things are of good report; if there be any virtue, and if there be any praise, think on these things.

–Philippians 4:8

Lord, so often we find ourselves asking you to save us from bad situations only to discover you quietly revealing to us that we are our own worst enemies! Teach us to break destructive habits and to stop polluting our minds with negative thoughts, Lord. Save us from our enemies, even when it means you have to step in and save us from ourselves!

October 19

Almighty God, I know you are supremely faithful! Today I ask you to restore hope to the hopeless. Plant seeds of hope in hearts that have lain fallow for so long. Send down showers of hope on those struggling with illness, persecution, or difficult relationships. Hope that comes from you is hope with the power to sustain us when nothing around us seems the least bit hopeful.

October 20

But the Comforter, which is the Holy Ghost, whom the Father will send in my name, he shall teach you all things, and bring all things to your remembrance, whatsoever I have said unto you.

–John 14:26

Thank you, Father, for your Holy Spirit, who guides me through each day. May I willingly follow his lead, no matter when or where. Help me to obey quickly when he directs me to serve or forgive others. May I always be thankful and rejoice in the blessings he points out to me along the way.

October 21

Lord, each day you furnish us with our daily bread. You feed and nourish us, yet often we neglect to acknowledge your gifts of food.

Forgive us, Father, for our selfishness and our disregard for your faithful care. We know that prayer should be a necessary part of every meal.

If, in our haste, we forget to thank you, Lord, remind us of our rudeness. Our meals are not complete until we thank the giver for his many gifts.

October 22

> *He that dwelleth in the secret place of*
> *the most high shall abide under the shadow*
> *of the almighty. I will say of the Lord,*
> *he is my refuge and my fortress: my God;*
> *in him will I trust.*
>
> *–Psalm 91:1-2*

Sometimes my doubts are so strong and so bothersome. Give me courage to express my doubts to you, O God, knowing that they are necessary moments through which I can pass on my way to true contentment in you.

October 23

> *This is the day which the Lord hath made; we will rejoice and be glad in it.*
>
> *—Psalm 118:24*

Look at the clock. What time is it? Is it time to go? Are we running out of time? I need more time! Lord, help me to stop and relax and enjoy time instead of feeling like it is my enemy. Help me be grateful for each minute and the special joys it brings. Sometimes I need to slow down and think of time as my friend. Thank you, Lord, for time and the gifts it brings me.

October 24

It's amazing how much joy an animal can bring into our lives. Today I am thankful for my pets—the ones I've had and the ones I know now. I am grateful for their love and companionship, and for somehow knowing when I need a hug or a cuddle. Sometimes it is good to just talk to animals and feel like they are really listening. Thank you, Lord, for the gift of animal companions.

October 25

Now the God of hope fill you with all joy and peace in believing, that ye may abound in hope, through the power of the Holy Ghost.

—Romans 15:13

We all have days when nothing goes right, and all we want to do is crawl back to bed and curl up into a ball. Sometimes those days stretch into weeks and months of bleak depression. But God is always there, watching over us, gently urging us to have hope because he has a plan for us. We may not see it unfolding, but it is, and hope is the pathway there.

October 26

> *Every good gift and every perfect gift*
> *is from above, and cometh down from the*
> *Father of lights, with whom is no*
> *variableness, neither shadow of turning.*
>
> *—James 1:17*

When I am thankful for what I have, I am given more. When I am not thankful, what I have is taken away. Gratitude is like a door that, when opened, leads to even more good things. But to be ungrateful keeps that door closed, and keeps me away from what God wants to bless me with. I am thankful, always.

October 27

*To every thing there is a season,
and a time to every purpose under
the heaven.*

—Ecclesiastes 3:1

You don't need to run a marathon. Just take one step at a time. Go out in faith and let God guide you. There is a season for everything, and God has perfect timing. Just listen and when he tells you to move, move!

October 28

*For ye have need of patience, that,
after ye have done the will of God,
ye might receive the promise.*

–Hebrews 10:36

We want it all and we want it now. But God knows better what is ours, and when we should have it. Relax and stop trying so hard! Let life flow and have faith that what is needed will arrive in good measure at just the right time.

October 29

Music fills my heart today! I am so grateful for music in all its forms: the loud thump of rock music, the pretty complexities of a classical symphony, the simple melody of a whistled tune. Thank you, God, for putting music into the world and letting it fill my heart with emotion.

October 30

Dear God,

I come to you today giving thanks for all the blessings you've bestowed upon my family. Even through the challenges, your presence has served to remind us we can get through anything with you to lead us. I am forever grateful for the love and grace and mercy you've continued to show us, and for the harder lessons we all have struggled through, and learned from. Knowing we have the love of God to light the way has been the glue that has held us all together.

Thank you, God. Amen.

October 31

Amidst hobgoblins and pranksters,
O God, we seek a quiet corner this
autumn evening to give thanks for
the saints whose day this really is.
Be tolerant of our commercialized,
costumed hoopla, even as you remind
us of the pillars upon which our faith
rests today. Keep our trick-or-treat-
ing fun, clean, and safe and our faith
memories aware, for it is too easy to
lose track of what we really celebrate
in the darkness of this night.

November

November 1

Your son, Jesus, was a reader, Lord. He read from your own books, the holy scriptures. Books can change us. They can transport us to other places and other times and can share the wisdom of the ages. I love books and reading and want my children to treasure them, too. Thank you, Lord, for good books, especially the Bible, that can feed our children's minds and imaginations and can show us the wonder of life in your world.

November 2

I will not turn back. I will not give up. I will never surrender. With God at my side, I will simply step over obstacles, go around challenges, and break through blocks put in my path. With God, I am unstoppable!

November 3

Thank you for our leaders. I might not always agree with them, but it is good to have people who will take charge and lead us. Help me remember to be thankful for those who dedicate their lives to public service, and help me to appreciate their vision of a brighter future.

November 4

A happy attitude is food for the spirit. Staying in
God's grace makes the challenges of life a little easier.
Lessons are learned with less effort.
Mercy is given more freely.
Joy returns!

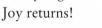

November 5

Holy God, you have shown me light and life. You are stronger than any natural power. Accept the words from my heart that struggle to reach you. Accept the silent thoughts and feelings that are offered to you. Clear my mind of the clutter of useless facts. Bend down to me, and lift me in your arms. Make me holy as you are holy. Give me a voice to sing of your love to others.

November 6

Life is filled with experiences that require us to reach deep within and find our courage. When fear threatens to keep us from trying something new, we can tap into that inner courage, which is God's presence, and find our footing. We may still be afraid, but we go forward anyway, knowing we will be given all we need to take on the challenge and tackle any new situation.

November 7

> *And the Lord shall guide thee continually,*
> *and satisfy thy soul in drought, and*
> *make fat thy bones: and thou shalt be like*
> *a watered garden, and like a spring of*
> *water, whose waters fail not.*
>
> *–Isaiah 58:11*

Father, I realize now that even people of faith have different struggles with discouragement and depression. It's a relief to realize that I'm not the only one. But where do I go from here? I need your wisdom and guidance. I guess this time of praying is the best place to begin. Just being reminded that you are near keeps me from the despair of feeling all alone, and it's comforting to feel so heard and understood when I'm talking with you. I need you to help me through this day, Father. Just this day. I'll take them one at a time with you.

November 8

Being confident of this very thing, that he which hath begun a good work in you will perform it until the day of Jesus Christ.

—Philippians 1:6

God, help me become a powerful loving presence in the world. Set before me directions to the path meant for me, a path that allows me to fully express your will through my words, deeds, and actions. Amen.

November 9

> *I delight to do thy will,*
> *O my God:*
> *yea, thy law is*
> *within my heart.*
>
> *—Psalm 40:8*

God, give me the insight to discern your will for me. Help me to ignore those who may not have my best interests at heart. Give me strength to stay on my own path until I achieve my goals.

November 10

I long to help every needy person in the world, Lord. Perhaps the most effective way to do this is by praying that you will send help wherever it is needed. Meanwhile, there is my corner of the universe with its many needs, and some of these are surely within my reach: half of my sandwich to the person standing near the freeway ramp with a sign; an evening spent going through my closet and setting aside items to donate; a weekend afternoon of helping with events at my church; a monthly visit to the sick, home-bound, or imprisoned. It's a privilege to honor you by extending your compassion—in person.

November 11

Thank you for our veterans and those who serve in the military. May I always remember those who have given up their day-to-day lives just to keep me and my country safe and secure. Help me to show my gratitude toward the veterans I meet and always remember to honor their sacrifices.

November 12

Why can't I be happy? I ask myself. The answer is simply, I can! Happiness is a day-to-day choice, not a by-product of a circumstance or an event like winning the lottery or getting a big promotion. There are plenty of miserable lottery winners, and numerous corporate executives suffer from depression despite their six-figure salaries. I can't buy happiness, and no one can hand it to me. It is a choice. It comes from within, and it is always available, just waiting for me to recognize it.

November 13

To let go is to live. Letting go opens the way for you to begin receiving more. Imagine a tree that refused to shed its dead leaves. Where would the new leaves find room to bloom forth in abundance? Without an outlet for new growth, eventually the whole tree suffers. By getting rid of the old to make way for the new, the whole tree benefits.

November 14

Therefore I say unto you, What things soever ye desire, when ye pray, believe that ye receive them, and ye shall have them.

–Mark 11:24

Prayer does not have to be formal and structured in order to be effective. Just sit quietly, let your mind be still, share your thoughts with God, and listen to the wisdom in your heart.

November 15

Dear Lord, we live in a broken world. We need your
touch. Heal us of our prejudices, our sicknesses, our
compulsions, our hatreds, and our shortsightedness.
Help us to see people as you see them. For that matter, help us see ourselves as you see us. Teach us to
treat life as the gift you meant it to be. Keep us safe.
Make us whole. Give us love to spare and forgiveness
that can only come from you. Amen.

November 16

Thank you for those who pray for me, Father. Thank you for putting me in their hearts and minds. I know that at times someone is keeping me in their prayers, and I haven't the faintest clue. It could be my hairdresser, chiropractor, pastor, or even someone I've just met. Perhaps a checker at the grocery store recalls a bit of conversation we had and now prays for me from time to time. You work in such unusual ways that I never know how it might be happening—I just know that it is so, and I am grateful.

November 17

Therefore being justified by faith, we have peace with God through our Lord Jesus Christ.

—Romans 5:1

Faith is the foundation upon which a happy, healthy life is built. The stronger our faith, the less our life can be shaken by outside occurrences and extraneous circumstances.

November 18

Cast me not off in the time of old age;
forsake me not when my strength faileth.

–Psalm 71:9

Lord, today I ask your special blessing on the elderly among us. No matter how old we are, we notice our bodies aging. How difficult it must be to be near the end of life and struggling to hold on to mobility, vision, hearing, and wellness of being. Give us compassion for those older than we are, Lord, and thank you for your promise that you will be with us to the very end of our days.

November 19

Lord, how grateful I am to have found the love of my life. May I never take her for granted. May I focus on her strengths and be quick to forget any silly disagreement. Help me to be her encourager and her friend as well as her lover. Protect the bond between us, Lord. Keep it strong, healthy, and loving.

November 20

How can I rejoice when I'm having "one of those days," Father? How can I pray continually when I feel overwhelmed?

When I look to Jesus' example, I find the answers I seek. He didn't stay on his knees 24/7, but he did maintain an ongoing dialogue with you. He acknowledged that he would prefer to avoid his cross, but he willingly took it up because it was necessary. He focused on the joy to come later, in due time.

I too can give thanks for the good things in my life, even when bad things are bearing down on me. I can keep up a dialogue with you as I go about my day, and I can be joyful in a deep abiding sense, knowing that all is in your hands.

November 21

For by him were all things created, that are in heaven, and that are in earth, visible and invisible, whether they be thrones, or dominions, or principalities, or powers: all things were created by him, and for him.

—Colossians 1:16

Creation shouts to me, Lord, about how amazing you are. I see the wonder of your wisdom in everything from the solar system to how bodies of water feed into one another to the life cycles of all living creatures. Everywhere I turn there is something that makes me think about how creative and insightful you are. Thank you for this universe that speaks without words. I hear it loud and clear, and it tells me of your magnificence.

November 22

*For all the promises of God in
him are yea, and in him Amen,
unto the glory of God by us.*

–2 Corinthians 1:20

When you say something, Lord God, it is as good
as done. It may not take place in the timing that
I'd imagine or wish, but you are true to your word
without fail. So when you tell me not to be anxious—but rather to pray and you will give me your
peace—I'll just do that. When you say that you
forgive me when I confess my sin, I'll believe that.
When you tell me that I'm your child and that you
rejoice over me, I'll take pleasure in that. Whatever you say, I'll not doubt it. Thank you
for your great and precious
promises and for your
absolute trustworthiness.

November 23

When I read this verse, I realize how perfectly Jesus personified heavenly wisdom. It's a wonder to me that we are called to walk in his footsteps, but then I remember that it is only possible to do it through the Spirit that works in and through us. Thank you, Lord, for making the things of heaven available to those who seek them.

November 24

And Jesus said unto them, I am the bread of life: he that cometh to me shall never hunger; and he that believeth on me shall never thirst.

–John 6:35

You truly do satisfy my spiritual hunger, Lord! In fact, when I'm away from you due to distractions or detours of my own making, I deeply feel the lack of you in my life. But then when I stop and take time to "feed" on your Word and spend time "drinking in" your comfort, I am strengthened and refreshed again. How true your Word is!

November 25

O Lord, as we enter this season of thanksgiving, how important it is for us to grasp the concept of "enough." You know how this world tempts us with all that is bigger, better—more in every way! But there is such joy and freedom in trusting that you will give us exactly what we need—neither too little nor too much. May we never take for granted all the blessings we have, Lord, and may we be as generous with others as you are with us. It is the simple life that brings us closest to you; we are blessed when we live simply.

November 26

Lord, today I pray for all those who have sought all the wrong kinds of protection. It's so easy for us to become obsessed with protecting our marriages, our children, and our well-being to the extent that we are in danger of losing our peace of mind. Remind us all, Lord, that when we are in your hands, we are in the best of hands. You will never fail us. You will never renege on your promises. With you, we stand strong and have great hope.

November 27

Today, in the dreary days as we head toward winter, I celebrate flowers. How wonderful it is to see their bright colors. I am grateful for the chance to bring flowers into my home to brighten a dreary day. Thank you for the colors and smells of spring and the opportunity to welcome them into my life at any time of year.

November 28

Father, there are many events in our lives over which we have no control. However, we do have a choice either to endure trying times or to give up. Remind us that the secret of survival is remembering that our hope is in your fairness, goodness, and justice. When we put our trust in you who cannot fail us, we can remain faithful. Our trust and faithfulness produce the endurance that sees us through the tough times we all face in this life. Please help us to remember. Amen.

November 29

Comfort me in my day of need with a love that is infinite and true. Ignore my lack of desire to forgive and forget. Fill my anger with the waters of peace and serenity that I may come to accept this situation and move on to a greater level of understanding and knowing.

November 30

O give thanks unto the God of heaven:
for his mercy endureth for ever.

–Psalm 136:26

His love is wider than our worries, longer than our loneliness, stronger than our sorrows, deeper than our doubts, and higher than our hostilities. This is why valleys are so wide, rivers so long, winds so strong, oceans so deep, and the sky is so high—with these, we can have a picture of the wonder of his love.

December

December 1

For the promise you unfold with the opening of each day, I thank you, Lord.
For blessings shared along the way, I thank you, Lord.
For the comfort of our home filled with love to keep us warm, I thank you, Lord.
For shelter from the winter storm, I thank you, Lord.
For the gifts of peace and grace you grant the family snug within, I thank you, Lord.
For shielding us from harm and sin, I thank you, Lord.
For the beauty of the snow sparkling in the winter sun, I thank you, Lord.
For the peace when the day is done, I thank you, Lord.

December 2

As I think of the people you've brought into my life, I think of the times and ways your light has shined brightly through me. I'm also aware of things I do and say, as well as the attitudes I have, that dim or obscure that light at times. Please trim the wick of my words, today; clean the glass chimney of my attitudes; and add the fuel of good behavior to this lamp that is my life in you. I ask these things for the sake of your reputation and to the glory of your Father.

December 3

God of all comfort, have mercy on me. I got angry today at my husband and accused him of not helping me enough. I scolded my child for talking too much. I shouted at the dog for barking too loud. And I almost hung up on my neighbor for taking up too much of my time with her plumbing problems. I need your comforting strength, dear God, wrapped around me like a soothing blanket, so that I can ask my family for forgiveness. Bless me with more patience, too, so that we don't have to go through all this again tomorrow. Thank you, God.

December 4

For what if some did not believe?
Shall their unbelief make the faith of God
without effect?

—*Romans 3:3*

Almighty God, our faith in you is undergirded by your faithfulness. No matter how many times we turn away, you patiently wait for us to return to you. Instill in us that same sense of honor and faithfulness that is yours, Lord. May we be as faithful to you as you have been to us.

December 5

Stand in awe, and sin not:
commune with your own heart upon your
bed, and be still. Selah.

–Psalm 4:4

Lord, it's wearying trying to be on the cutting edge,
working to "be somebody," scrambling to get to
the top of the mountain first. Sometimes I need
to pull away from the rat race and be quiet; to put
away my goals, appointments, and lists and just be
with you, Lord. I crave the peace of your presence,
and I need to feel held by you. Please pick me up
and let me lean against your heart, which I know is
full of love for me and all the world.

December 6

God, a call, a note, and a handclasp from a friend are simple and seemingly insignificant. Yet you inspire these gifts from people we have a special affection for. These cherished acts of friendship nudge aside doubts about who we are when we feel low and encourage our hearts in a way that lifts our spirits. Thank you for the friends you have given us.

December 7

> *To the Lord our God belong*
> *mercies and forgivenesses, though we have*
> *rebelled against him.*
>
> *—Daniel 9:9*

Do not worry about the regrets of the past. God forgives you. Do not stress over a wrong word or a misguided action. God forgives you. Do not cry over a bad decision or a terrible mistake. God forgives you. Learn the lessons from your actions, then turn to God and know that he loves you and forgives you. Then strive to do better the next time.

December 8

Sometimes it is difficult to appreciate snowy weather, but I thank God for the gift of snow days. How wonderful it is for everyone to be home, safe and warm. On snow days, life returns to a simpler pace and the demands of schedules and responsibilities fall away. Thank you, Lord, for the beauty of the snow and the time it gives us to relax and share quiet times with our loved ones.

December 9

O Lord, what a blessing it is to worship during the Advent season and prayerfully consider the joyous celebration of your birth. Don't let us get so bogged down by minutiae that we miss the miracle, Lord. Prepare our hearts as we prepare our homes and families for Christmas, and help us keep our focus not on everything we need to do, but on you.

December 10

The glory of the Lord shall endure for ever:
the Lord shall rejoice in his works.

–Psalm 104:31

Father, I am so grateful that your thoughts and your
ways go so far beyond my own! Things in my life
can be going along smoothly—and I may think I have
everything under control—but it can all change in the
blink of an eye. Help me stay connected with you,
Lord, so that whether I'm enjoying smooth sailing or
enduring high seas, I'll know I'm held fast by you.

December 11

In these nutrition-infomercial times, prepare me a table of pleasurable moderation. And, Lord of salads and sundaes, assure me that nothing in your creation is itself bad; as always, it's what I do with it that determines its value. Be with me at the smorgasbord.

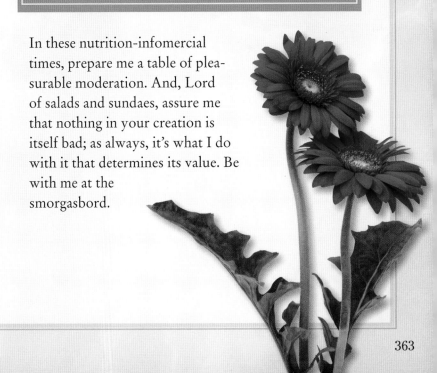

December 12

And I will establish my covenant between me and thee and thy seed after thee in their generations for an everlasting covenant, to be a God unto thee, and to thy seed after thee.

—Genesis 17:7

Father, I often need these assurances of your concern for me. Thank you for stating again and again in your Word that you love me and are looking after my well-being. Help me to take you at your word today and, in childlike trust, have confidence that you are always near.

December 13

Shopping, wrapping, traveling, cooking. So much
to do this season as we hurry toward the manger,
answering God's call as did those folk so long ago,
to go, believe, and do. Practice the notes of the carol,
for soon it will be time to sing out "Gloria!" at what
we'll see and hear.

December 14

O God of justice, we confess that we are too quick at times to judge those around us, basing our opinions not upon what is written in their hearts but what is easily seen by our lazy eyes. Keep us faithful to challenge one another any time we find ourselves speaking in generalities about any group of people or repeating jokes and slurs that offend and degrade. Remind us that all of creation bears the imprint of your face, all people are children of yours, all souls are illuminated by your divine spark. We know that whatever diminishes others diminishes your spirit at work in them. Make us respectful, humble, and open to the diversity around us that reflects your divine imagination and creativity.

December 15

Lord, sometimes I feel guilty that I haven't thanked you enough for the blessings in my life. I know I possess luxuries that others merely wish for. In this cold month of December I am grateful for the roof over my head, the heated seats in my car, and the warmth of my family and friends. Remind me not to take these kindnesses for granted and help when I see someone in need.

December 16

I've heard it said, "You're only as sick as your secrets." God, give me the courage to present all of myself to you, all of the time. The good and the bad. Although you can read me like a book, I feel shame when I keep things from you. Help me to open myself up. Thank you, God.

December 17

Not by works of righteousness which we have done, but according to his mercy he saved us, by the washing of regeneration, and renewing of the Holy Ghost.

–Titus 3:5

The past, O God of yesterdays, todays, and promise-filled tomorrows, can be an anchor or a launching pad. It's sometimes so easy to look back on the pain and hurt and believe the future may be an instant replay. Help us to accept the aches of the past and put them in perspective so we can also see the many ways you supported and nurtured us. Then, believing in your promise of regeneration, launch us into the future free and excited to live in joy.

December 18

Wings of light surround me,
And I am enlightened.
Wings of love enfold me,
And I am comforted.
Angels guide my journey,
And I am directed.
Angels keep me safe from harm,
And I am protected.

Arms so strong lift me,
And I am emboldened.
Arms so soft hold me,
And I am at peace.
Angels grant me mercy,
And I am redeemed.
Angels walk beside me,
And I am esteemed.

Songs of joy fill me,
And I am enchanted.
Songs of love envelop me,
And I am empowered.
Angels sing above me,
And I am adored.
Angels chant in glory,
And I am restored.

December 19

Let me do what lies clearly at hand, this very minute. Grant me the insight to see that too much planning for the future removes me from the present moment. And this is the only existence, the only calling I have been given—right now to do what is necessary. Nothing more, nothing less. Thus may I use this next moment wisely.

December 20

Lord, I'm getting nervous as we prepare to welcome
family into the house. I don't want to see any sparks
fly between any of my siblings or our extended
family. Uncomfortable conversations about politics
or how we raise our children can make for unhappy
holidays. Please guide us in your way so that we may
wisely do your bidding.

December 21

Thank you for my community. As I run my errands and conduct my business, let me remember to be grateful for everyone who helps me. From a clerk at the store to the police officer keeping me safe, my community is filled with people who help others. Thank you, Lord, for putting these people in my life and for giving me the chance to know them. May I always work to make my community a better place.

December 22

Dear heavenly Father, I truly want to do good toward others. I don't want to just talk about being good, but I desire to be more compassionate. God, I need for you to teach me to be far more sensitive to the needs and sorrows of the people you have placed in my life and to be kind and encouraging toward them. I need for you to teach me how to truly love. I pray for this with all my heart. Amen.

December 23

Loving Father, help us remember the birth of Jesus, that we may share in the song of the angels, the gladness of the shepherds and the wisdom of the wise men. Close the door of hate and open the door of love all over the world. Let kindness come with every gift and good desires with every greeting. Deliver us from evil by the blessing which Christ brings and teach us to be merry with clean hearts.

December 24

Tangled in tape, lists, and holiday wrappings, we are all thumbs of excitement! Bless the surprises we've selected, wrapped, and hidden. Restore us to the joy of anticipation. We want to be surprised, too. Our wish lists include the gift of peace possibilities, of ears to hear a summons and eyes to spot another's need or triumph, of being able to make a difference. As we cut and tape, God of surprises, remind us to keep in touch with the gift's recipient after the wrapping papers are long gone and the ornaments packed.

December 25

Merry Christmas! Thank you, Lord, for this special day. It is the birthday of your son, Jesus, and a bright and beautiful day for the world. Today I am grateful for rebirth, for celebrations, for sharing traditions with the people I love. Thank you for the gift of joy and new life.

December 26

Herein is love, not that we loved God, but that he loved us, and sent his son to be the propitiation for our sins.

–1 John 4:10

Lord, how grateful we are that our spirits don't have to sag once the excitement of Christmas is over! We don't want to be like ungrateful children tearing through a pile of presents just to say, "Is that all?" For the gift you gave us at Christmas, your beloved son among us, is a gift that is ours all the days of our lives and throughout eternity! Thank you for the greatest gift of all, Lord.

December 27

Lord, as I clean out closets and make lists for the New Year, show me any "gods" I have placed before you. Help me to look honestly at how I spend my time and my money. Does one of these areas of investment reveal a strong allegiance to something other than you? If so, Lord, help me eradicate those distractions from my life once and for all.

December 28

Loving God, how many times have I resolved to spend time first thing each morning in your Word and in prayer—and how many times have I neglected to do so! A day that begins with you, Lord, is sure to be a day blessed by you. Give me an insatiable thirst for time with you, Lord. And thank you for always being available to meet with me.

December 29

When we see our enemies from God's perspective, compassion follows, for he has seen the sorrows in their hearts that have caused them to behave in such a manner. He longs to reach out to these people and comfort them, and he sometimes uses our hands to do it.

December 30

We have seen that inconceivable acts can cause our world to crumble around us. Yet we need not fall apart inside. If we place our trust in God's goodness, he will come to our aid and bring us comfort to restore our hope in the future. His love and compassion will lift our spirits so we can rejoice no matter what disaster or tragedy may befall us. For as long as God is beside us, nothing can defeat us or take what is truly important from us.

December 31

The calendar is as bare as the Christmas tree, the page of tomorrow clean and ready. May God bless the New Year that beckons, helping us face what we must, celebrate every triumph we can, and make the changes we need. And now celebrate to the fullest this whistle-blowing, toast raising moment, for it is the threshold between the old and new us.